Six Essential Elements of Leadership

PUBLISHED WITH THE MARINE CORPS ASSOCIATION

Six Essential Elements of Leadership

Marine Corps Wisdom of a Medal of Honor Recipient

COL. WESLEY L. FOX, USMC (RET)

Naval Institute Press
Annapolis, Maryland

Naval Institute Press
291 Wood Road
Annapolis, MD 21402

Library of Congress Cataloging-in-Publication Data

Fox, Wesley L.
  Six essential elements of leadership : Marine Corps wisdom of a Medal of Honor recipient / Col. Wesley L. Fox, USMC (Ret).
     p. cm.
  Includes bibliographical references and index.
  ISBN 978-1-61251-024-8 (hbk. : alk. paper) — ISBN 978-1-61251-067-5 (ebook) 1. Fox, Wesley L. 2. Leadership. 3. United States. Marine Corps—Military life. 4. United States. Marine Corps—Officers—Biography. 5. Vietnam War, 1961–1975—Personal narratives, American. I. Title. II. Title: Marine Corps wisdom of a Medal of Honor recipient.
  UB210.F66 2011
  658.4'092--dc23

                                                                                      2011018581

♾ This paper meets the requirements of ANSI/NISO z39.48-1992 (Permanence of Paper).
Printed in the United States of America.

 24 23 22 21 20 19 18 17   15 14 13 12 11 10 9 8

Jacket image: Colonel Fox flanked by HM2 Charles "Doc" Hudson, USN (left), and PFC Al Albertina, USMC. (Official U.S. Marine Corps photo)

THIS BOOK IS DEDICATED TO THE MARINES OF YESTERDAY

WHOSE PERSONAL SACRIFICES

DEMONSTRATED THE LEADERSHIP TRAITS ADDRESSED IN THIS WORK.

Contents

Preface

Leadership is intangible, and therefore no weapon
ever designed can replace it.

General Omar Bradley

When James McGrath suggested *The Six Essential
Elements of Leadership* as the title for this book, I considered one change: adding the word "positive" to the
title. But if leadership isn't positive, it isn't leadership. If
a leader's methods or techniques aren't working or influencing and inspiring others for whom he is responsible,
it isn't leadership. If the team isn't accomplishing the
mission or objective, leadership is missing. If the person
responsible for mission accomplishment isn't at the same
time taking care of those who will actually accomplish the
mission for him, it isn't leadership.

Many great leaders in the past have provided guidance
on how to handle and conduct the task of guiding, motivating, and leading others. Their thoughts and experiences
expressed in the written word convey important, timeless
messages, and I quote some of them in this work. Captain
Adolf von Schell, for example, wrote articles and gave
presentations on his varied leadership experiences during
his service with the German army during World War I.
He related the lessons he learned as a small infantry unit
commander, and his observations and thoughts are still
valuable today.

Other writers have written about and reprinted von
Schell's work, the latest being Major Edwin F. Harding in
1933. Major Harding's work was reprinted by the Marine
Corps Association in 1982. This excellent book, *Battle
Leadership*, is available today to Marines. I quote von
Schell's thoughts on the source of leadership: "To be an

officer means to be a leader—to be a leader of troops in battle. It is certainly correct that great leaders, like great artists, are born and not made; but even the born artist requires years of hard study and practice before he masters his art. So it is with military leadership; if he is to learn the art of war, he must practice with the tools of that art." I'll address his point that leaders are born, not made, later.

There are other good books on leadership that will help those wanting to know more about the art of influencing others. Major General Perry M. Smith, USAF (Ret.) provides a down-to-earth guide with his great book *Rules and Tools for Leaders*. He teaches leadership at Canon, Texas Instruments, and Microsoft. I have worked with General Smith at Auburn University's Blue Ridge Conference on Leadership conducted in Black Mountain, near Asheville, North Carolina, for several years now. The conference is a very positive gathering of managers and assistant managers who wish to better understand what is expected today from leaders.

Colonel Don Myers, a friend and fellow retired Marine, wrote *Leadership Defined*, a book that covers the subject nicely by using his experiences in the Marine Corps and in business after his time in uniform. Don and I were together in George Company, 3rd Battalion, 5th Marine Regiment in Korea in 1954–55, and he was my escort to the White House for my Medal of Honor presentation in 1971.

One of the Marine Corps' best sergeants major, Alford L. McMichael, provides his thoughts on achieving life-changing success from within the person, the individual. He wrote his book, *Leadership*, which I strongly recommend future leaders read, after he retired from active duty in the Marine Corps. McMichael, however, doesn't tell his full story in his book. I was very much impressed with his manner of handling daily office business, along with being receptive to his friends and peers who might visit him, while we served together at Marine Corps Officer Candidates School in Quantico, Virginia.

McMichael's office was across the small passageway from my office door in the headquarters building. His office was very hot in summer and cold in winter. If it was really hot and humid outside, his windows were wide open. It was the same in winter; on the coldest days his windows were up. He never used the air conditioning or heat. McMichael's purpose was to keep the bull sessions in his office to a minimum. Other senior staff noncommissioned officers might come by to say hi, but they didn't stay long, and that was McMichael's purpose. He had work to do, and most of it, or at least his interest, was outside in the field with the candidates, running their courses with them and observing the individual performance of his sergeant instructors.

Michael Useem's book *Leading Up* furnishes interesting thoughts on the importance of leaders working and communicating with those in higher positions over him or her. Leading other people works in both directions, up as well as down. Hans Finzel's book, *The Top Ten Mistakes Leaders Make*, impressed me. Finzel makes good points throughout, and I quote his work several times. Finzel notes that future organizational leadership will be of the flat type. He discusses the embedding of responsibility, accountability, and authority at all levels in great detail.

I served with and knew many good and even great leaders during my time of active duty with our country's supreme fighting force, the United States Marine Corps. I learned much from my fellow Marines in this regard, and I pass on to the readers of this book what I gained throughout those years. I enjoyed forty-three years of providing personal, positive leadership. Yes, forty-three years: My squad leader in the Korean War moved me into one of his fire-team leader positions in only my eighth month in the Marine Corps, so all of my Marine years involved leading fellow Marines. My platoon leader promoted me to corporal the following month, and it has been all down-hill movement (meaning easy) ever since.

In the following pages I discuss how my superiors and fellow Marines impressed me with their manner of guiding, directing, and leading others, their followers. I also lay out my personal thoughts on leadership and what it means to me. My six essential elements of leadership are just that: Good leaders have, build on, and exercise all six elements; a shortage in one requires extra effort and concern for the others. The bottom line is that I learned that when I was directly involved with my Marines, when I would look them in the eye and tell them, "This is what we want to accomplish," we got it done. And distance, as in rank or position of the leader in reference to his followers, does not have to be a barrier. I was never a general officer, but I know Marine generals who were always very much involved with all ranks of their commands. For me, the rank of colonel never kept me out of the trenches or from being directly involved with my Marines. I loved it.

Acknowledgments

Writing a book of my experiences in my Marine life never entered my mind until my later years. I was aware some Marines kept diaries, especially in combat, and when asked about them would state that maybe someday they would write a book about their Marine experiences. But not me; that was never my interest. Now here I am with my third book. What happened? Well, these days writing is easier than running three miles in eighteen minutes, swimming from a submerged submarine four thousands yards offshore through rough surf, or jumping out of airplanes. Also, this book concerns my favorite subject, leadership, a matter in which I was directly involved for fifty-one years. I know a little bit about it and thought I could pass on knowledge that would be helpful to someone down the road of life in their relations with others.

I would like to thank James R. McGrath for suggesting that I write my thoughts about and experiences with leading Marines. He also suggested *The Six Essential Elements of Leadership* as the title of the book, which I liked immediately. Another factor that influenced me to write this book was the realization that I had already written part of it for my leadership presentations. All I had to do was include the words and thoughts from my speech manuscripts. I love to talk on leadership and often get invited to do so at Marine professional military education (PME) programs. Jim McGrath checked in on me and my progress periodically, and he provided much help with his thoughts and suggestions on the manuscript. Bing Swain also provided interest in and input on my work. Although it has been years since they wore the uniform, both are Marines.

I gained much from other authors who expressed their thoughts about leadership. These authors and their books are recognized in the Sources section of this book. Leaders and those desiring to be leaders would do well to have these books on their library shelves.

SECTION I

Leadership

Leadership Defined

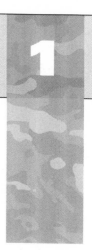

Leadership effectiveness is what you learn
after you know it all.

John Gardner, Leadership

Has the high technology involved in all aspects of our daily lives today replaced the requirement for personal leadership within our society and our armed forces? Has the immediate availability of several types and levels of communication and observation reduced the need for leaders or made them not as important to mission accomplishment today as they were in the past? Small, fully capable computers might have some of the needed information regarding a situation available with the touch of a finger. Many of our modern weapons, such as remote-controlled bomber and fighter aircraft and precision-guided long-range missiles, do not require hands-on control. (I will address this issue in the following chapters.) My answer to the above questions is we need leaders at all levels and in all situations. Times may have changed a leader's manner and methods by which he exercises guidance and control, but there will always be a need for leadership.

A friend, a Marine colonel, retiring from active duty shortly after being passed over by the brigadier general selection board, described what top leadership is all about during his retirement ceremony speech: "I decided to retire from active duty because my daddy always said, and my feelings are, that if you aren't the lead dog, your view is always the same." Right on. He makes a valid point. I suppose this isn't saying much on the positive side for the mid-level leader who has that thing waving in front of his or her face, but it could be considered motivation for advancement; good, strong leaders want to be the lead dog.

What is leadership? Webster describes leadership as the "capacity to lead." I looked up "lead" in the dictionary and found "positioned at the front" and "having the initiative." Still not satisfied, I looked up "leader" and found "person who directs a military service or unit, a commanding authority or influence." We all acknowledge and recognize leadership within our armed forces, and that last word, "influence," fits with my thoughts of children and the family. Mom and dad's leadership is an everyday childhood experience and a treasure in our homes and within our society.

For most of us, our parents were our first leaders, or they should have been. There was obvious leadership involved in my childhood, though at the time I didn't recognize it or rate it as such. As the oldest of ten children, I should have, and did have while growing up, the opportunity to exercise a little leadership on my own. But this seldom, if ever, happened; I was too involved with self.

My dad was there, the rock, and I knew from experience what to expect from my screwups, and they were plenty enough. As I got bigger, older, my mother's punishment changed to "Just you wait until your daddy gets home!" That was enough to get me back on the straight and narrow. Family leadership is over the long haul, and those leaders are, from the start, part of the educational process of leading others. While I learned much from my mom and dad, I really learned grass-roots leadership from the Marines.

Many parents have a rough row to hoe in our society today when it comes to raising children—in spite of an easier way of life, meaning with all of the modern comforts in the home, automation at all levels, and our physically less-demanding means of travel. Modern comforts mean to this yester-year farm boy that one doesn't start his day by getting up in an unheated house on a cold morning in January, building a fire to heat the kitchen, going outside to use the outhouse, and breaking the ice in the water bucket for water to wash one's face. Or, while mama cooks breakfast, going to the barn and milking four cows, by hand, and all of this before the school day or work day starts, seven days a week. Maybe modern-day comforts give people more time for thoughts and concerns for self. Some people, it seems, have a problem with their individual commitments to others, including family members, and their neighborhood.

My thoughts here may well fit in the "Care" and "Personality" chapters of this book because the person is the issue, and the problem is one's manner of recognizing, respecting, and dealing with the other person, someone who is breathing one's air, maybe in one's air space. But my opinion is that the real issue is our society, the people of today who have a different perspective on others and whether or not to recognize their needs. Again, I see the focus on self: "I am all that counts!"

I have read that our society is full of "me first leaders and don't ask me followers." Here the message is that the "me first leaders" are not focused on situations such as being the first off the landing craft onto a hostile beach such as Iwo Jima, the first in an assault on an enemy position, or any other dangerous or difficult situation. They want to be first in all creature comforts, first in the chow line, and first on the list for any and all personal comforts and benefits. And of course this kind of leader fits right in with the follower's "don't ask me" mentality. We as a nation are fortunate in the fact that these types of individuals are few and far between.

Groups and masses of people need someone in charge, someone to make the decisions regarding all people, someone who will do the right thing in the best interest of everyone. A leader or several leaders are needed to provide guidance in doing what is in the best interest of all people involved in or influenced by a situation. And therein is our problem. An example is our inner cities. Yes, there are mayors and others, including police forces concerned with and providing guidance to some extent, but at the lower level, on the streets, with little or no guidance from parents, leadership is sorely missing.

Our major interstate highways illustrate the fact that many people today are self-centered and focused on *me*. I see this every time I'm on the road: "It's mine for my use as I desire!" Here we have many people using the same commodity at the same time with almost no one on hand for guidance as to what is in the best interest of all. Each individual has had his or her exposure to road rage. How do we get leadership on our highways? In most cases the only authority is the highway patrol, and these officers are too few to be of much help. The truck-congested interstate highways make my point of what happens without leadership.

Fifty years ago the highways belonged to everyone and we all shared them. Specifically, truck drivers were friends to those in need on the road. I knew that I could count on their help. You broke down, had a flat tire or whatever, and the next trucker coming along stopped to see how he could help. People in general shared the road and respected other drivers on the road.

Today that trucker is after another mile on his paycheck. How many times have you and fifty other cars crept behind an eighteen wheeler while the truck's driver passed another truck going a tenth of a mile slower than he? Long, steep grades are the worst; that trucker is going to get in the passing lane and hold up the traffic all the way to the top: "To heck with the other person, I am all that counts. Me and another forty-four-cent mile for the day."

Not all truckers fit that mold of course. Some truckers move at a safe speed and pretty much stay in the right lane as they maintain the posted speed limit.

Drivers for companies such as Yellow, England, Roadway, J. B. Hunt, and H. T. Harris don't fit the above negative comments. Leadership is obviously involved with these truckers, and I'm sure there are truckers working for other good companies I haven't named.

What about truckers playing lane control? "I am in charge of this road; no cars will get ahead of me." They see signs indicating that there is a lane closure ahead, yet miles from the closure, with bumper-to-bumper, stop-and-go movement, a trucker positions his rig beside another truck to stop forward movement in the passing lane. All the way to the closure that lane cannot be used—except behind that truck. A mile of the lane ahead of him is wasted, not used. His immature purpose is to keep all of those automobiles from getting ahead of him. He is not smart enough to realize that cars easily fill in the spaces ahead of trucks due to a truck's slower movement in starting forward from a full stop. Time and roadway would be better used with filling in the gaps. This truck driver control of the road ought to be against the law in all states.

Another useful law in all states would be to require all trucks to move at the same speed, fifty-five miles per hour on all interstate highways. They have replaced railroad trains, after all, and they should move as trains, one line, one behind the other, no passing. Several of our central states (Illinois and Indiana are two) do limit truck speed on their interstate highways to fifty-five, and that greatly reduces the line of backed-up automobiles behind trucks in the passing lane.

But it is not only truckers who don't care about the other guy, the other driver. Being of the old school and showing care and concern for the other person, when I come up behind a slower mover, I don't move left into the passing lane if my rearview mirror shows an automobile closing at a faster speed. I wait until it passes, then I move left. Many times others have moved into the passing lane as I approached from behind only to cause me to brake and follow at a much slower speed while they pass at the speed of an all-day venture. Eventually they move back into the right lane. Maybe.

Other examples of the focus on self on the highway are those car drivers who move at a slower speed in the passing lane and remain there. To heck with the roadside signs that read "Keep to the right except in passing" or "Travel in right lane, pass in left." These people make a big statement of just where other people rate with them as they slow many other vehicles to their much slower speed. No, it isn't a safer speed, not when they create the traffic block and 90 percent of the vehicles must try to get around them on the right. Too many times the vehicle on the right is moving at the same slow speed. There is absolutely no thought, care, or concern for the other people. It is all *me*.

We need leadership on our highways. How do we get that? It starts in the state capital with laws that are considerate of all needs. A few more uniforms on the road would be a big help, too. Large groups of individuals without leadership are lacking in guidance and motivation. The issues outlined above are not going to improve without some work by our lawmakers. As our population increases, so will our conflicts. The only solution is to get leadership on our highways with applicable laws and the enforcement thereof.

You must start with a study of human nature if you desire to involve yourself in leadership. You must place yourself in the positions of those whom you would lead in order to have a full understanding of the thoughts, attitudes, emotions, aspirations, and ideals of your people. A wanna-be leader can learn much from those in leadership positions over him, focusing on those leaders' actions that motivate him and cause him to want to be involved. Making a leader is addressed in a later chapter.

The leader's primary concern should be the morale of his unit or organization. Having the right morale, people can do what was thought impossible. Great morale can replace the shortage or lack of material things, and who should know that better than a U.S. Marine? The Marine Corps during my early years was always short on gear and equipment, and in many instances our weapons had already served many Marines earlier. It was a hand-me-down environment, but we had the spirit and we made do with what we had.

My battalion commander in the Vietnam War, Lieutenant Colonel George W. Smith, often expressed to us, his company commanders, what he believed leadership is all about, at least in our Marine Corps. I heard him state a number of times, "Teach, train, guide, and take care of your Marines, including their families to the degree that you can, and they will charge right up the enemy's gun barrel for you in a moment's notice and never ask why." I love that expression, and it is so very true of Marines and their leaders, at all levels. I think of leadership as being able to influence others to reach deep down inside themselves and pull up that something they didn't know they had. Real, positive leadership has to be before us, provided, and active during the really tough times that face us, especially when death is a possibility.

We all agree that leadership is caring for, guiding, directing, motivating, and inspiring others, especially those for whom we are responsible. If leadership is so important to each of us, to our communities, to our society, and to our country, where can one study how to lead his fellow man? Where can one get an education, a bachelor's degree in something so important to us? (Don't even think of a master's or a doctorate degree in leadership—not in our United States.) Of course our military services are very much involved in studying, teaching, and exercising leadership, but even our military academies do not offer a bachelor's degree in leadership.

The meaning of leadership to Marines has always been that the leader knows his people; he knows the details of what is going on, he is involved, and he is up front with the action, especially in combat. In Vietnam, as in all wars, that meant living with the same handicaps, environment, life threats, and enemy situation as one's people. Bad weather meant to the rifleman in Vietnam, for example, that there would be no flying of helicopters for medevacs, resupply of ammo, or water and rations. We all lived it, from the top commanding officer down to the rifleman.

Our situation got so bad in the A Shau Valley on Operation Dewey Canyon due to the extremely high heat and no chopper flights to bring in water and rations that the war dogs were evacuated. Imagine that! The environment and our situation was too tough for our dogs but not for Marines. The dogs could not live out there in that jungle, in the heat and without water. Marines hung in there and, of course, paid a price. That is the Marine Corps: "The difficult we do immediately; the impossible takes a little longer."

I am of the opinion that there are basically two types of leaders from the follower's viewpoint. Both will have their positions of leadership identified by an office, position, or a uniform with rank insignia, but that is only part of it. One will exercise his authority through his position, concerned only with result and anything that will make him look good. My drill instructor in boot camp in 1950 fit this model. He really didn't care about me personally, and that fact was easily read; he was there to do a job, and he ensured that his people (recruits) didn't get in his way. Physical and verbal abuses were at his pleasure. The fact that he was not interested or concerned with us was expressed in several ways, not the least being his restriction on drinking water. His mentality was "Get tough; learn to do without water!" The following event helps make my point.

After several hours on the drill field on a very hot afternoon in August, I was very thirsty for water. We weren't provided with canteens; the only place we got water was at the scuttlebutts (water fountains) in our barracks. Well, I wasn't familiar with the word "dehydrated," but I knew I needed water as we, over and over, tried to get our close-order drill right. This amounted to flanking and column movements, marches to the rear, and cadence count, with the commands repeated over and over. Our utility uniforms (field dress for Marines) were completely soaked with sweat; even my socks were sopping wet. I had to have a drink of water.

Finally, we headed for the barracks, and I realized that I would be the first in the barracks and at the scuttlebutt. Some of my fellow recruits had gotten a drink in the past as we rushed into the barracks, even though we were told not do so. The drill instructor always followed the last recruit in, so there was no issue. I would get water. Our platoon was halted in front of our barracks, and following a "Right, face," Corporal Reiser stated, "When you are dismissed, I want you standing tall in front of your racks. Dismissed!" I was off like a streak, the first recruit inside and at the scuttlebutt. Just as the cold water hit my lips, Corporal Reiser's voice sounded very closely behind me: "Shithead, I didn't tell you to drink water." I was already moving when his boot caught the seat of my trousers, and I was surprised that he didn't follow me to my rack. Of course I was moving very fast.

Bottom line on this type of leadership: If he wasn't around, I would do for that kind of a leader what I knew he wanted done only if I knew he would learn that I had the opportunity to do so and didn't. If he wasn't around or near me, he wasn't my leader; he had no influence over me or my thought process.

The other type of leader from the follower's perspective is the one who cares about his followers, goes out of his way to do and provide for them, and sends the message in many positive ways how his subordinates rate with him. My squad leader in the Korean War was this kind of a leader, and I relate accounts of his leadership in this book as well as in my memoir, *Marine Rifleman: Forty-three Years in the Corps*. My point here is that I would do for my squad leader anything I thought he might want done. If I felt that he would want something taken care of, it was done, whether or not I thought he would ever learn of my doing or not doing the act and regardless of the cost to me, physically or otherwise. *People* are what leadership is all about. A leader takes care of them, does for them, and is always concerned for and involved with what is in their best interest. This fact is easily read and understood by the followers.

I recognized real, positive leadership in the Korean War. Though I was familiar with the subject, as I mentioned earlier, from family and friends, my squad leader really impressed me with what leading others was all about. Because he was so good at handling us in that tough combat environment, I relate some of his leadership examples here, even though I provide his full story in my memoir. There is no better example of leadership. Leaders just don't come any better.

Corporal Myron J. Davis, USMC, was my squad leader in the Korean War, and he was my first leadership mentor. I later handled those Marines for whom I was responsible just as Corporal Davis would have done. He caused me to think about the end results: Where are we going with an issue and at what cost? Where do we want to end up and in what condition? What is in the best interest of my Marines, my squad, and the Marine Corps?

In a later chapter, I relate examples of several shortfalls that Marine infantry experienced in the Korean War due to problems in higher-level national as well as Marine Corps leadership. These shortfalls were not caused by Corporal Davis but at much higher levels, starting with our president and his belief that there would be no need for infantry fighters in the future. Corporal Davis helped us get through the tough times in spite of these shortfalls.

Corporal Davis, my squad leader (3rd Squad, 3rd Platoon, Item Company, 3rd Battalion, 5th Marine Regiment, 1st Marine Division) in the Korean War, impressed me from the start, and he grew in stature with each passing day. John Wayne, for his role as Sergeant Stryker in *Sands of Iwo Jima*, could have learned much from my corporal. A soft-spoken Marine from Pocatello, Idaho, he was my first mentor in the demanding role of leading Marine riflemen in combat. Because of our respect for him, his first name was always "Corporal" until it later changed to "Sergeant." (At that time most corporals were addressed by their first or last name with no rank.)

Davis had a long, blond handlebar mustache that was an immediate clue as to how long he had been in combat. Otherwise, in those days Marines did not wear hair on their face. He had a .38-caliber revolver tied low down on his right thigh. The pistol had belonged to a Marine buddy of his who had been killed as they carried out an assault across the Han River just out of Seoul. Davis' purpose was to ensure that the pistol was returned to his buddy's father, who had mailed it to his son. Davis said he didn't trust the rear-echelon people to send it; the pistol would end up in one of their sea bags. My point here is that he didn't wear it for looks.

As we knocked out and destroyed the enemy bunkers in our assaults on ridgelines in Korea, Corporal Davis usually would be the first Marine inside the bunker following the explosion of our clearing grenade. After a while, I became concerned because I realized just how important Davis was to me and my fellow squad members. I didn't like the thought of us losing him, of having to do without him. So I, Private First Class Fox, approached the corporal one day, saying, "That was my job!" The Browning automatic rifleman is trained and expected to be the first in the bunker, firing as he moves in. Davis responded with, "Look, Fox, how much quicker I can turn this pistol to cover an unexpected threat in a corner of the bunker compared to you turning that heavy, long-barrel rifle." That was a good point, and before I could think of a counterargument, like "Give me the pistol," he stated, "And no other hand will touch this pistol." End of subject.

I cover in a later chapter my thoughts regarding leaders moving forward and doing the rifleman's job and subjecting the unit to the greater chance of being without their leader, especially an aggressive leader, warrior, and gunfighter. While there are no doubt situations in which this action is justified or is a positive action that can help win a battle, the possible loss of a good leader is a high price to pay. Corporal Davis' bunker action no doubt had a major part to play in my later recognition of how devastating the unnecessary loss of a leader could be to a unit. I would have been forever getting over his loss—a loss that occurred while he was doing my job.

We, the members of 3rd Squad, knew that Corporal Davis cared about us. He never used that four-letter word "love," but his every action expressed it. Little things like C-ration issue were a daily reminder of how we rated with him. At that time C-rations came with three meals to a box, about the size of a shoe box. Our problem was that we were always in the assault, taking one ridgeline after another, and we didn't need the extra weight of a day's rations of canned food. My Browning automatic rifle and magazines of ammunition weighed forty-one pounds; add to that the weight of two grenades, cold-weather clothing, a backpack with personal items, and a sleeping bag, and I was already overloaded. I didn't need another five pounds of food added to my load. So we were issued one meal for the assault and would be resupplied on the objective once it was secured.

The problem was some of those meals were not fit to eat. Corned beef hash, ham and lima beans, and sausage patties with gravy, for example. Three of us would have to share a box; who gets what? "Hell! I had that hash yesterday. I want the beans and franks today!" We would almost fight over a meal. Corporal Davis always issued all meals to his three fire-team leaders with instructions to give him the meal that was left. I surely hope he liked corn beef hash, because that is all he ever got. His Marines were always first in his thoughts.

My corporal made another strong statement of his concern for his Marines. I don't know what the Marines earlier that winter had for a food-heating source in the Frozen Chosin. But in my time, from January to June 1951, our only means for thawing out and heating our C-rations was a wood fire. (We didn't get the little heat tabs for C-rations until June of that year.) Well, we had no chance to build a fire in the mornings because we were moving forward in the attack shortly after daylight. After taking our objectives, our first priority was digging our fighting holes followed by clearing the fields of fire. By then it was usually dark, and one doesn't build a fire unless one wants to show the enemy where to drop his mortars and artillery rounds: "Here I am, drop it on me!"

Consuming our food the majority of the time meant chipping the frozen stuff out of the can with a bayonet. While in this environment one night, I heard Corporal Davis state, "I am going to get a Coleman Burner even if I have to carry it." The next time we moved back into regimental reserve, Corporal Davis showed up with a Coleman stove that he had gotten from some Army unit. And true to his words, he didn't add that weight to my load or to any of his Marines. He carried it. In spite of carrying the stove, he never used it until all of his Marines had finished with it. He loved coffee in the mornings, but many mornings we were moving before he had a chance to make it. He was our leader.

The best example of Corporal Davis' performance in leading Marine infantry in combat happened after the rains started. The cold, hard winter was softening up for us; we had rain instead of snow, our first rain since my arrival in Korea. We had been on the attack for days through rough terrain, and we had had little sleep, with a 50 percent watch each night (this meant for the two Marines in a fighting hole, one was awake at all times, with one hour of sleep followed with a one hour watch throughout the night) and poor rations. (We were provided with C-rations, but the problem was thawing them so they could be eaten. This was before Davis got the stove.) Then came the rain. It rained all night. The next day, there was no word on continuing our attack forward, no word to saddle up. Maybe we were going in reserve, we thought. We badly needed sleep, rest, and food. We stood around soaked with the rain and cold, waiting. There were no fires for heating our rations because the wood also was soaked.

Finally, word came down for us to saddle up. We were being relieved by an Army unit. Item Company Marines moved off the line, their sleeping bags and clothing thoroughly soaked. Besides the misery of being physically exhausted, hungry, wet, and cold, the rain-soaked gear added much to the weight on our backs. But that was almost unnoticeable because we were moving rearward down the ridge. Great!

With high spirits, we moved down the back side of that ridge, thinking of the hot chow; of long, uninterrupted sleeps, maybe in tents; and of letters from home waiting for us. We were all on a high with everyone talking about what we were about to enjoy. However, at the bottom of our ridge, we turned left, moving to the flank and parallel with the main line of resistance (MLR). It was clear to all of us that we were once again being committed to take an objective that some other unit could not handle or hold, one the higher commanders felt would be under an enemy assault and they couldn't afford to lose. We plodded along knowing that the situation was only going to get worse; there would be no hot chow, no sleep, and no letters.

Our squad morale was dangerously low. Personally, my spirit was right down in the mud with my feet because of my weakened physical condition. I have never been so down and so demotivated. I realized that I really no longer cared about anything. Tomorrow was too far off to even enter my mind. I would never see it. As we plodded along, I felt that it was all over for me; I couldn't do any more, my end was coming up.

Thinking these negative thoughts, a voice seeped into my consciousness. Someone was singing. After my initial disbelief, I tuned in Corporal Davis singing, "Never saw the sun shining so bright, never saw things going so right." The words did not fit our situation, and I resented the implication. Then I realized that I really had to listen closely to hear the words. The corporal was not making a show of his singing. He was not being a smart ass. He had read correctly the loss of our team spirit, our morale, and our desire to continue on. Obviously, all the Marines felt as I did.

How did Davis read this low morale situation within our squad? Of course he no doubt had the same feelings of exhaustion and loss of spirit, but his concern was his Marines, and within his squad there was complete silence—no talking, no one even bitching. And that is a heavy, bad signal to Marine squad leaders. If your Marines aren't bitching, you have a major problem.

My thoughts shifted to "I know his game; this is all part of leadership. He is just trying to make us feel better, raise our spirits." I refused to be influenced. My spirit would stay in the mud at my feet. We trudged on, and the words and tune continued, not forced or obnoxious, but audible if I listened closely enough. Our gloom gradually faded. Someone back in the file made a remark, more of a loud bitch, and a little farther down the trail someone responded to the bitch. Shortly, we were all talking, even if it was bitching. The squad spirit returned, and we moved into night bivouac ready to do what had to be done the following day.

My corporal had come to Korea with the Maintenance Company of the 1st Provisional Marine Brigade in August 1950. A refrigeration repairman by military occupational specialty, he was later assigned to Item Company as a rifleman replacement for the casualties taken during the Pusan Perimeter fighting. Davis was an example of our Marine Corps commandant's desire: every Marine a rifleman. He was with Item Company for the amphibious assault at Inchon, the attack through the city of Seoul, the Wonsan landing, and the fight out of the Chosin Reservoir.

There were two other brigade Marines in our squad, but they had rejoined the squad after being wounded and spending months in the Navy hospitals in Japan, where they had a break from the everyday life of the infantry Marine. When I arrived, Davis was the only 3rd Squad member to have gone through it all. He experienced many nights the wonder if he would see the light of another day. His focus and interest were never of himself. Regardless of the difficulties encountered, his focus was always on his Marines, his followers.

Corporal Davis had all of the essential elements of leadership, and he continually exercised them. We, his squad members, learned much from him and his manner of handling us. Davis is proof that one person can make a major mental contribution to others with whom he is involved.

Leadership versus Management

Name me an industry leader who is thinking creatively about how we can restore our competitive edge in manufacturing. All they seem to be thinking now-a-days is getting themselves bigger salaries and bonuses.

Lee Iacocca, Where Have All the Leaders Gone?

All over the country, in corporations and government agencies, there are millions of executives who imagine that their place on the organization chart has given them a body of followers. And of course it hasn't. It has given them subordinates. Whether subordinates become followers depends on whether the executives act like leaders.

John Gardner

The above quotations address my purpose with this chapter very well. Subordinates and followers are people; what is the difference between the two? People are the most important resource/asset that we have to help us accomplish our mission in both our civilian world and our armed forces. Do we lead or manage people? To which do they, the people, more quickly respond, leadership or management? In this chapter we consider the difference between the two.

Many institutions of higher learning offer all sorts of degrees in management, but fewer than a dozen colleges and universities in our United States offer a degree in something as important to our society as leadership. Does this problem have to do with the difficulty in or inability to identify leadership? Or is it the complexity of correctly placing leadership within either the social science or art field? Robert Taylor and William Rosenback address this issue in their book *Military Leaders*: "The leader, to bridge that last gap between corporate management and true leadership, still depends on the un-measurables, that is, on art rather than science. The elements of his gift, or his skill and how he develops it, are qualitative rather than quantitative, and the problem for the humanist describing the leader is that he is trapped by the inadequacies of the language to describe qualities that defy precise definition."

The authors recognize Harvard psychologist David McClelland's study, which resulted in the finding that managers in organizations need power, not achievement, in order to be strongly associated with success. The authors continue: "Organizations are set up because there is work to do that can't be done by just one person, that requires people to work together to achieve goals. The process is controlled by the exercise of power and influence. Managers who have an extremely high need to achieve tend to burn out; they get frustrated about things not getting done and try to do everything themselves. But that is not really possible; in large organizations, people must use influence and rely on others to get things done."

The above thoughts express the basic problems involved in recognizing and handling management and leadership. How does management fit with leadership in our everyday sense or use of the words? Webster defines management as a judicious use of a means to accomplish an end. There are many degrees available in management, and management itself covers a broad area. So broad, as a matter of fact, that we are a nation full of managers. Anyone with a title of any importance is usually a manager of this or that. He manages both people and things in accordance with Webster's definition. To many managers, people tend to lose their personalities, their human aspect, and become the "means." Most managers' involvement with their means, the people known as "subordinates," includes hiring, firing, harnessing, directing, and driving them.

Management in today's environment is concerned with cost, production, and profit. A manager's aim is to get the most for the buck. The high-tech cost of doing business today demands such if a business is to be successful; cost is always a concern. Some of these earlier money-making business managers, however, are now showing another side, or direction, to their management, especially CEOs in the top positions of organizations such as banks, U.S. automobile makers, Wall Street firms, and others. These top-level managers have rewarded themselves personally with millions of dollars each year, even though their businesses have been sliding downward. Where is leadership expressed in a state governor who attempts to sell a vacated U.S. Senate seat for money? He is just another "me first" leader, the issue amounting to "more money for me." State governors and top-level managers must be leaders; they have to have the leader's integrity, the leader's personality. Because of the shortage of these personal traits, however, personnel in top management positions must have eyes on them and their official actions. There must be someone in a position to say no. The lack of personal integrity is the big issue with these individuals, and that is our society's problem today. Our society acts as though there is one big gray area between what is right and what is wrong. And if the supposed number-one leader surrounds himself with yes-men, he has an open road to do as he desires.

The problem, of course, has to do with not being mentally prepared to handle the position, responsibility, or obligations of being number one. The situation is somewhat similar to my first year as a drill instructor at the San Diego Marine Corps Recruit Depot. I was it; I was right up there beside God, and anything I wanted to do with my recruits, I did. There was no one around to say no. But after six recruits drowned in the Ribbon Creek incident at Parris Island, South Carolina, in 1956, drill instructors received on-hand supervision. During my second year on the field, I received many no's and was often told, "You can't do that." All leaders and managers need checks and balances to their official activity.

Compare the quality of some of today's business management with what I have addressed in chapter 1 on leadership. What is the major difference between the two? Can management get the job done while also being concerned for the workers? Is there a need for leadership? If so, where?

I see leadership as being people orientated. People need, and leaders provide, guidance, inspiration, motivation, and education. A good leader can cause others to reach deep down inside themselves and pull up that which they never knew existed. Leaders cause people to step outside of their personal world of desires and self-gratification and do for and be involved with others. They cause people to be concerned for the personal good and welfare of others, for the team, and for our society.

Webster's definition of leadership, noted in chapter 1, needs amplification, because leadership is more than directing. Managers direct. And Webster's "commanding authority" only goes so far because it too comes with the office or billet (commanding officer, mayor, president). Many of those who have filled these positions under these titles have fallen far short in leadership, in setting a good example, in doing for and being concerned about their subordinates, the people for whom they are responsible. Authority might start with the office or the uniform, but leadership goes much deeper. The office and uniform are only the outer shell; leadership involves that which is within the person.

The leader is a teacher, not only in job performance but also in the whole-man concept. He helps to improve mankind and our way of life by guiding and helping the individual. He helps subordinates establish and attain goals while ensuring fair and equal treatment to all on the job. He directs and encourages his followers to seek and maintain personal physical and mental health. Management can get the job done regardless of the cost to an individual employee's future health, but leaders are concerned about their people beyond the job's output, concerned about their health, concerned about the whole person, including his or her family.

We are all aware of people in high political positions who should have exercised leadership because of their potential influence on the people of our country. Some have not done well, while others have left office in disgrace. Some have talked the talk, but when faced with the walk, they have fallen far short. In most cases, we see these fallen people as guilty of one or more violations of proven leadership principles. They fell in disgrace because they gave in to personal greed, to satisfying their personal desires and needs over what was good for the team, the people. Is this weakness in our political and judiciary "leaders" brought on because we as a nation do not teach our young people leadership in our educational system? Would a genuine leader of people ever respond to a question on his or her personal, negative conduct with words such as "It depends on what the meaning of 'is' is"?

While leadership comes naturally to some, such as my squad leader in the Korean War, Corporal Davis, we who aspire to be involved with people need to be aware of the requirements of leadership. Addressing and studying the principles of leadership and the traits of a leader are a start. But leadership goes much deeper. Over the years I have come to understand that the word "care" is the difference between leadership and management.

Care and concern for subordinates mark the leader; the subordinates of such a leader become followers. Management does not necessarily care about the people hired and fired; they are only the means. They, the individuals, usually can be easily replaced, and depending upon the employee's time with the organization, maybe at a much lower cost or salary. A leader has to care. This care is shown by actions, not words, and is easily read by the subordinates, who return this care with similar action and motivation, expressed in their spirit, in this living thing called "esprit," for their purpose. Leaders, not managers, deal with and are concerned with esprit. Leaders create and maintain esprit in the hearts of their people.

One of our Marine Corps' past great leaders, Major General John A. Lejeune, wrote, "A good leader must be able to play upon the emotions of his people in such a manner as to produce that most wonderful of all harmonies—the music of the human heart attuned to great deeds and great achievements." He continues: "Morale includes physical as in professional, mental as in spiritual, and esprit de corps." The general broke esprit out of his mental-spiritual category because of its importance to morale. As I understand his order of these factors, mental things include instruction, training, and, in general, those things that can be taught. Esprit, on the other hand, is the spirit of the people, of the troops. Being of the spirit, Lejeune notes, esprit "is intangible, imponderable, and invisible. Esprit cannot be perceived by any of the five human senses, but nevertheless, every leader knows that it does exist and that it is the most potent of the forces that are necessary to utilize in order to achieve victory." The general goes on to explain that education assists but little in building esprit, that it is a matter of dealing with the emotions, the spirit, the souls of the people. Reading these words, the reader can understand why Marines are so good in the performance of their warrior duties. Their leaders inspire esprit, to a very high degree, in each and every Marine.

All organizations need esprit to excel, to beat the competition. To win is what esprit is all about, whether it is winning in battle, in sports, in providing a service, or in producing a product. Case in point: Who would you rate with the highest esprit, the employees of the U.S. Postal Service or those of United Parcel Service? Which of our airlines? Federal Express is at the head of the list on organizational esprit, and it is a positive, forward-moving organization. Why? How did they achieve this? Their organizer, director, and leader, Fred Smith, is a Marine; I would bet that fact had a major play in Federal Express' success. Fred Smith understands unit esprit, has lived it, knows how to build it, and knows what it gives you in return.

Leaders are responsible for stirring up the spirit of competition between organizations. All great organizations have had one or more great leaders who, in his own character, was the incarnation of the aspirations of his people and who, in his turn, built up their morale and esprit and led them to their goal. The leader must embody in his own character the virtues that he would instill in the hearts of his followers. True esprit de corps is founded on the great virtues of unselfishness, self-control, energy, honor, and courage.

Again, to borrow from the wisdom of General Lejeune, the relationship of a leader and his subordinates should be that of a father and son, exercising the same care, concern, respect, and guidance. This relationship makes the follower one who will accomplish the mission, regardless of the difficul-

Leadership needs management. All organizations need management in order to judiciously use the means to accomplish the ends. However, people, including managers, need leadership because leaders create followers, thus motivating the members of the team. The better the leadership, the more perfect the leader, the better the followers. Let us teach and train our leaders of tomorrow in the essential elements of leadership.

Sources of Leaders

3

Without leadership, change is unintentional. With leadership, people come together and decide collectively and deliberately whether and how to institute change. No subject is more compelling or worthy of study.

Dean Sandra Peart, Jepson School of Leadership Studies

Today's leaders, of both our nation and local societies, must recognize the need for leadership and work out the "hows" of its development. We have plenty of young people who will, as they mature, gladly take on the role of leading others. They, however, must learn the basics, and where do they do that? Where does one acquire the art of inspiring and positively influencing others? I feel that the desire to be a leader is a personal commitment for those who want to make a difference in their community and society.

Leading the list of personal commitments should be the commitment to one's spouse and children. Our society today does not prepare young people well for that commitment—a total commitment to the person chosen as a lifelong companion. Today, it seems, a contract is made between two people and later that contract is broken. It is as simple as that. There is little serious thought to the consequences of the loss of the mother-and-father team leadership to the children, the young lives who have to struggle on without that unity. Yes, usually these moms and dads are available to their children and involved with them individually, but they are no longer working together as leaders of the family team.

Family leadership is a matter of devotion and commitment. One's commitment to his or her spouse is not dependent only upon love and all that the word means to most of us. A qualification for a commitment in marriage is not "love at first sight" or "this the only person in the world for me." None of us would be so naïve or gullible as to believe that we somehow found the only person in the world who could be our mate, that of all the people of the opposite sex in the world, half the human population, we just happened to find the one and only. What is required is love and commitment. We have to, and do, work for what we want. A marriage between a man and a woman works only because each of them wants it to. Each goes a little further for the other, does things in the other's interest, shows that he or she cares. Our marriage vows should mean something to us other than just words stated for a formal occasion. "Until death do us part" means just that to me.

If things aren't going right in a relationship, then one if not both members of that relationship must get to work. Usually, however, most of the problem is with one side; one of the mates does not go the extra distance in trying to make the marriage work. I know of several marriages in which one spouse sticks it out and continually goes above and beyond what the other spouse does in contributing to an atmosphere of love within the family. One spouse puts up with all of his or her mate's nonsense, lack of attention, lack of care, and lack of family involvement and tries to make the marriage work. And that spouse's purpose is keeping the family team together for the children's sake, at least until those children grow up and leave home. By the time the children leave home, the good mate, the one who has put up with the other's nonsense all of this time, says, "Enough" and they separate. The negative family member probably didn't contribute much to the children's learning of positive leadership because those children were no doubt constantly exposed to the negative parent's lack of commitment, dedication, care, and true love.

A person who does not lead himself well is doubtfully going to come across well in filling a leadership role in front of others, including his or her children. Total commitment means our involvement with those things we want badly enough. And a good home life with love and care expressed daily by a mom and a dad, total commitment by both parents, is something all our young citizens deserve. Leadership is needed within the family, which in turn is a springboard for great leaders within our society, politics, our armed forces, and our nation. A great benefit passed to children from good parents is the awareness that they, the children, control or at least have a direct influence over their own destiny. They will be only as good as they want to be. In this regard one is never too old to be as good as one wishes to be, never too old to start to have a positive influence over his or her destiny.

It is just too easy in our society today to shuck our family leadership responsibilities and move on to other personal interests. Yes, some of those don't work out either, but here there is usually a major personality problem involved. In other words, if not both individuals then at least one has a problem with people relationships. It is not my purpose to address that issue here but to recognize that the great majority of second marriages and relationships work.

How and why? I suppose it becomes easier to recognize what is needed in a relationship having gone through it all once before; this experience gives one the knowledge of what to do and when to do it—as well as all of the items on the do-not-do list. If those involved in a second marriage had done the same thing, had maintained the same interest with the same care in their first marriage, that one also would have worked.

Another point—as the first marriage involves the majority of our children—is that the first marriage is the one to work hardest at keeping together, if only for the children's sake. Of course some people learn from their mistakes, and some do better their second time around, but think of the loss of constant, everyday love and positive leadership that the children suffer. In his song "Holding Things Together," Merle Haggard addresses my point well: "When it comes to raisin' children / It's a job meant for two."

As noted above, leadership really starts in the home, though in many individual situations it isn't recognized as such at the time. Our moms and dads provide the guidance, motivation, and direction in our lives as children and move us (hopefully) in a positive, forward direction. They are also the disciplinarians; they correct us and provide the punishment for our indiscretions. Parents are responsible for preparing and leading our future individual society members and leaders on the correct road to health and happiness. But this way of thinking fits more with yesterday than it does today.

In my growing-up years during the 1930s and 1940s, all the children I knew had one parent at home. It was usually the mom, and she was there with that daily guidance, advice, and punishment (if necessary). We, the children, always knew that mom was in the home for us, that she would handle any situation in which we needed her involvement. Home leadership began to change with World War II and the opportunity for work, which meant more family spending money. Of course many of the men were away and in a military uniform; the war required such. The war also laid a heavy hand on manufacturing business, and our women were asked to help out. Our society and country situation has continued in that direction every since. We have fewer mothers in our homes during the day, fewer family leaders available at any moment to handle the issues confronting our children on a daily basis. In some cases our children are left to work it out themselves or to be influenced by the advice of another kid who knows no better. In some of our homes, leadership is missing until evening, when mom and dad return from work; in other homes, it is missing completely.

I do not want to come across as too negative regarding our modern-day society. It is true that a lot of our young people's problems are caused by the lack of parental leadership, but many working mothers today do provide that same care, concern, love, and leadership for their children. Ladies involved in business, medicine, law, politics, and other enterprises have a heavy schedule on their professional shelf, but they work it out. With the help of a warm, loving secondary mom in the home when mommy has to be in the office, all bases are covered. Involved and concerned mothers are in the home as soon as possible and for the remainder of the day. The majority of today's mothers have covered their children's needs and home life extremely well with the same leadership and love I experienced as a child.

As a young Marine, I was aware of military leadership in its many and varied forms, including leadership provided by supposed leaders who didn't motivate me to follow them. If I had options to do otherwise, I probably did not follow, at least closely. Others, who were real leaders, did motivate me, and I would follow these leaders to the very gates of hell. The awareness of and the motivation to lead others comes early in life for most of us. Here I will address leadership involvement at a younger age level and within our country's educational system.

The armed forces as well as military schools are great sources for learning leadership. By starting out as a follower, you have the opportunity to observe and learn from those in leadership positions. Those leaders you like, who please and impress you, are the ones after which you will style your own leadership. Young people, our future leaders, tailor their leadership actions so that they fall in line with their mentors' ways of handling them.

Our active armed forces and the military academies, including schools and universities with Reserve Officer Training Corps (ROTC) programs, make leaders. After I retired from active duty in the Marine Corps, I accepted the position of deputy commandant of cadets at Virginia Polytechnic University in Blacksburg, Virginia. I continued to be involved with leadership as I worked with cadets in their movement upward and their goal of leading others. Most of my time was involved with providing guidance and direction to the upper 10 percent of cadets, who were in leadership positions and had heavy loads in addition to their academic schedule. Much time was also spent trying to get the lower 10 percent squared away mentally and physically or out the door. The experience was educational all around and a real motivator for me.

The experience with the Corps of Cadets also helped me adjust to the fact that I was no longer an active-duty Marine, a fact that had caused me some serious thoughts several years earlier when I learned that one could not serve on active duty forever. "How am I going to handle the fact that I am no longer a real, live, kicking Marine?" I asked myself. "Retire where? Do what?" I had earlier missed the fact that the Marine Corps Manual states that one can not serve after age sixty-two without a waiver from the president of the United States. The cause of my ignorance was the fact that I knew of no other dummy who wanted to spend his entire life in the Marine Corps. The issue had never come up. What a bust when I learned of the age sixty-two mandatory retirement constraint.

I remember back in the 1950s, as a sergeant in the Armed Service Police, Washington, D.C., hearing Chief Warrant Officer Bales (referred to by all of us as "Pappy" Bales) state, "Today I have thirty years in the Corps; think I'll make a career of it!" Pappy looked like he had been in the Corps forever; two wars will do that to a person. I quoted Pappy's statement twice, for my thirtieth and fortieth years in the Corps, and at forty-three years, I still intended to make a career out of the Marine Corps.

The Marine Corps was downsizing in 1993. Young Marines had no choice but to depart the ranks upon the end of their enlistment or commission contract, so I didn't have much of a chance to stay in the Corps. Why keep an old guy around when young warriors have to leave? Another touchy point: I wouldn't ask the guy filling the commander in chief's slot in 1993 for anything. So I departed the ranks quietly.

Virginia Tech's Corps of Cadets made my transition into retirement easy because I still wore the Marine uniform, I was concerned with haircuts and shoe shines, and leadership was the name of the game. General Carl Mundy, the commandant of the Marine Corps, gave me a personal letter authorizing me to wear the Marine uniform in retirement with the Corps of Cadets. My days were really no different from those of my last several years on active duty as the commanding officer of the Marine Corps Officer Candidates School (OCS) in Quantico, Virginia. We were making leaders, and leadership was our daily activity focus.

Virginia Tech's Corps of Cadets has a great leadership program and rewards those desiring such with a minor in leadership upon graduation. Hopefully, in the not-too-distant future, graduates will walk across the stage and receive a major in this very important field. But as of this writing, that degree, in spite of its importance to our society and our country, is not available at Virginia Tech.

The Jepson School of Leadership Studies at the University of Richmond in Richmond, Virginia, is the one institution I know of that awards a bachelor's degree in something so important to us all, our society and our country. I was surprised to learn from Sandra Peart, the dean of the Jepson School of Leadership Studies, during my visit with the university that there are about half a dozen other institutions throughout our country that offer a bachelor's degree in leadership. I was not aware of this fact and was pleasantly surprised. But why are there so few? Is leadership so hard to teach? Are there so few high school graduates interested in learning leadership that the field of study is not worth an institution's efforts and expense? Could the problem be a lack of motivated and qualified instructors? I doubt both of those thoughts.

The point I want to make here about the Virginia Tech Corps of Cadets is that those desiring the training and the knowledge required to successfully lead others receive the full package. Students' four years as cadets start out with his or her first year as a follower, pure and simple. The freshman is the lowest element on the totem pole, and they are made keenly aware of such. Their daily plight and endeavors reminded me of my Marine Corps boot camp days at Parris Island, South Carolina, in 1950. My DI (drill instructor) constantly reminded us of just how low we, his recruits, were. His favorite line was that we were "lower than whale feces," and that was on the very bottom of the ocean. Of course Corporal D. W. Reiser didn't use the word "feces." One cannot be placed much lower than that.

In their second year, as sophomores, cadets move into leadership positions at the small-unit level, as team and squad leaders. As juniors they move up to the senior sergeant positions—platoon sergeants, first sergeants, sergeants major—and staff positions within the battalion and regimental headquarters. As seniors, they are officers; they are the commanders at all levels, from regimental commander down to platoon commanders, including all staff officer positions. By their fourth year cadets are ready and do a great job in leading, motivating, and guiding the force. They have worked three hard years for the opportunity, learning leadership all the way.

The Corps of Cadets has three battalions of cadets with a retired military or naval officer, rank of 0-6 (Army, Marine, or Air Force colonel, or a Navy captain), known as a deputy commandant of cadets, leading and managing each battalion. I had the 1st Battalion for eight years; eight more years of leadership training with young Americans, eight more years in a Marine uniform added on to my forty-three years of active Marine duty. I loved it, every day of it, the physical fitness tests, the obstacle course (an official, regulation Marine Corps obstacle course that I had the Roanoke Marine Reserve Combat Engineer Company build for us), the long humps (field marches), and the runs. My greatest pleasure was working with young people wanting to be involved with providing guidance, direction, and motivation to others.

Another important point about the Virginia Tech Corps of Cadets is that 80 percent of these graduating cadets are commissioned into our armed forces each year through the Reserve Officer Training Corps. This percentage is about double the number other university corps of cadets, such as those at the Virginia Military Institute, The Citadel, and Texas A&M, commission through their ROTC programs.

What really impressed me in my time with the Virginia Tech Corps of Cadets was those individual cadets working for and deserving the top cadet leadership positions. The very best cadets each year were awarded the top command positions following the Command Selection Board's recommendations and a thorough study of the cadet's past record (board members were retired military officers working for the Corps of Cadets). Past cadet commanders' written evaluations of the subject candidates were also closely studied; only the best qualified received the command positions.

My battalion commanders for my last three years at Virginia Tech were females. They were selected by the Command Selection Board as best qualified. Not only were they best qualified as shown throughout their two years in small-unit leadership positions, but they were extremely motivated to tackle the job, to take on the responsibility of higher-level leadership. Each of them did a great job at commanding and leading others. They were the best commanding officers overall that I had during my time with the Corps of Cadets, and I have no doubt about that. Their involvement with others was their choice, their desire, and they were motivated to lead. They each wanted the responsibility of leadership, the opportunity to do for others, to take charge and get thing accomplished. And they did.

What follows is a recommendation I wrote for one of my female battalion commanders. It helps make my point of just how good our best cadets are in these command positions.

06 October 2000

To: Selection Board, Who's Who Among Students in American
       Universities and Colleges
From: Colonel Wesley L. Fox, USMC (Ret) Deputy Commandant of
       Cadets, Corps of Cadets, Brodie Hall, Virginia Tech, Virginia 24061

Letter of Recommendation for Gina ————

I have known Gina for the three-plus years that she has been a cadet at Virginia Tech. She has easily managed the stress of combining academics with our demanding military lifestyle, and she has excelled in both areas. Her warm, sincere personality fits snugly within the framework and ideals of the cadet corps, causing her to stand out among her peers as a leader. A caring concerned person, she extends herself readily to others. Gina is a doer, one who gets involved and gets things done. She participates in all corps activities and volunteers for the extra assignments regardless of the demand on her personal time. Gina has sought and been selected for leadership billets within each of her year-groups, from a motivated freshman with a "can-do" attitude to Team Leader as a sophomore followed with Battalion Sergeant Major as a junior and a Battalion Commander during her senior year. This year she is also the Head Resident Advisor for Brodie Hall.

Gina's other cadet achievements include leading an organization named Female Cadet Encouragers that has the purpose of providing support to new females within the male dominated corps. She is a member of the Arnold Air Society and the Civil Air Patrol, a key member of the Corp's Retention and Recruiting Staff, and a participant in the Cadet Leadership Conference. Gina was involved with the past summer's Orientation/Recruiting Program conducted for prospective cadets. She has also served as the Public Affairs Officer for the Air Force Group.

Gina's scholarships include the Corps' Emerging Leader and the Air Force ROTC. Other awards and recognition include an excellent rating upon completing the Air Force field training, two Corps of Cadet grade awards, Cadet of the Month for January 1999, and Honor Flight for Spring 1999. She has increased her physical fitness to the point of recently achieving a perfect score of 500 on the Air Force Physical Fitness Test.

I have worked with many cadets and students during my eight years with Tech, to include eight battalion commanders. I do not hesitate to state that Gina stands out above all as a leader, as a cadet, and as a person. She is a true example of UT PROSIM [That I May Serve], and I recommend her with enthusiasm for your selection as a Who's Who in American Universities and Colleges.

Sincerely,
Wesley L. Fox

TEACHING POINTS FOR MY CADET COMMANDERS

The following points were presented and discussed with new commanders in reference to our getting ready for a new school year and the incoming freshmen, the followers.

How to Motivate New Cadets

- Create a desire to be a member of your team
- Create a feeling of belonging to the team
- Work with cadets having problems
- Show "how to do it" by the numbers (some of us are slower at catching on)
- Sweat with your new cadets, meaning be involved with them
- Praise in public, call attention to weakness in private

What Not to Do Because It Demotivates

- Mass punishment
- Criticize in public
- Call attention to continued individual foul-ups
- Punish unfairly
- Show favoritism
- Demean by name, race, sex, or desires

To Have Meaning to Cadets, an Order or Action Must Have Purpose

- What is the purpose of the new cadet's year?
- Training in close-order drill, physical fitness, being a member of the team
- Screening and evaluating leadership potential
- Level all personalities to a common denominator
  - How? By stress, fatigue, confusion, and the unknown?
  - This one could bite us—what is the justification?

The Evaluation of Your Work, Your Job as the Commander, Is Based upon the Final Outcome or Results of Your Company of New Cadets

- How many have you lost?
- What are your company's disciplinary problems and what is its motivational level?
- Are you approachable with a problem?
- What is your purpose here at Tech?
- Did the cadets kicked out of the Corps serve their purpose?
- Keep in mind—each new cadet arrives here wanting to do well. Build on that.

Some Unique Leadership Thoughts Provided in a Cadet Leadership Class

- Your availability in the Corps of Cadets is as important as your ability.
- Your personal actions are so loud that I cannot hear what you say.
- Will alcohol help you gain your lifetime objectives?

General Perry M. Smith emphasizes the point that making a leader is a continuous process in his book *Rules and Tools for Leaders*. After the desire to be, after the schooling and training, and after the assignment, leadership begins. The general writes, "Leadership is not synonymous with authority. It is, to a very considerable extent, a value that is entrusted to superiors by the associates or subordinate leaders. It embodies an emotional, often spiritual investment—a gift of trust. To a great extent, the associates define the conditions under which trust is given. They prescribe the qualities, characteristics, and values that the superior must possess in order to be fully accepted as the leader. It is a wise leader indeed, who understands and nurtures this relationship between leaders and followers, especially with the followers who may not be very visible."

Young Americans desiring to be leaders today have several institutions where they can gain the required experience and education. The armed forces are in the forefront with the Reserve Officer Training Corps, and involvement with ROTC also helps with the higher educational financial load. Hopefully, more universities will offer a degree in leadership to those desiring such. There is certainly a heavy need for positive leadership. Businesses need leaders for the forward guidance of the managers. Our national leader source should be unlimited.

Principles of Leadership

4

If your actions inspire others to dream more,
learn more, and become more, you are a leader.

President John Quincy Adams

The U.S. military's register of the Principles of Leadership has been around a long time, and it is as meaningful today as it was when it was first presented about one hundred years ago. I cover each of these eleven principles throughout this book because they outline exactly what leading people is all about. These principles define the makeup of our best leaders. To fall short in exercising any one of them is to fall short in an important element of the principles required for leadership.

THE PRINCIPLES OF LEADERSHIP

Know yourself and seek self-improvement
Be technically and tactically proficient
Seek responsibility and take responsibility for your actions
Make sound and timely decisions
Set the example
Know your people and look out for their welfare
Keep your people informed
Develop a sense of responsibility in your subordinates
Ensure that the task is understood, supervised, and accomplished
Train your people as a team
Employ your unit in accordance with its capabilities

I cover in a later chapter some of the difficulties I endured in my first leadership position, when I was placed in charge of Marines who at that point had spent more time in the Marine uniform than I. Although that statement is not quite correct because as Marine Reservists they had only worn the uniform for one evening a week and two weeks every summer. (This was before reserve training changed to one weekend per month.) They had gone through boot camp training, so we were even on that count. Nevertheless, my leadership experience started out on a very rocky road because of my fellow fire-team member's resentment of my elevated junior (boot) status over them. (I also had a youthful appearance at the age of nineteen, which didn't help me impress these older Marines with my ability to be their leader.)

The other Marines' salty behavior toward me, however, only lasted until our next big firefight. At that point these older boys were satisfied to let someone else assume the responsibility of deciding what to do and when to do it—or take the blame for what wasn't done correctly. By the time I returned to my squad after being wounded in our squad's assault on a North Korean army machine-gun position on 8 June 1951, these old salts were no longer in Item Company. I never learned what happened to all of them; several of their names, along with mine, are on the casualty list in the archives of the Marine Corps Historical Center for the action on 8 June. The others found safer duty elsewhere or an easier way home. Most of them were activated Reservists and were not committed for a full combat tour of duty in the Korean War.

Upon my return in the latter part of June 1951, I found our 3rd Squad, 3rd Platoon, Item Company made up of 100 percent young Marines fresh from infantry training following their boot-camp training in the states. I was immediately aware of a major difference in the individual motivational level with the Marine "can do" attitude. Because of my time in the Corps, eleven months all total at this stage, our platoon leader, Lieutenant Brimmer, made this boot corporal the squad leader of our 3rd Squad. Great, I thought. Now I could be a little Corporal Davis. (Davis had completed his combat tour and left us as a sergeant back in May and returned home to the States. The Marine Corps was in better shape personnel wise at this time, and Marines within units committed in Korea during August and September 1950, and who had fought in the Chosin Reservoir battles, were being sent home several months short of a year in Korea.)

The United Nations forces had ceased their assault northward at or about the thirty-eighth parallel in late June 1951. Peace talks were under way, and our mission was to hold in defensive positions. The only activities we had were patrol actions: a platoon combat patrol every third day and a short, close-in squad reconnaissance patrol the two days in between. The only threat of enemy action was at night. This situation was short lived for me (about ten days) when our Marine division was pulled off the line and assigned the mission of Corps reserve. This was the only time we received this division mission during my ten months in Korea.

Here is where I got my first stand-alone, top leadership position, meaning there was no one looking over my shoulder, telling me what to do and how to do it. This assignment gave me the opportunity to study and exercise the Principles of Leadership seriously, and I intended to ensure that I was not short in any one of the principles. For the next two weeks I rated myself in regard to each of the principles and considered how I might improve. I knew that I had a long way to go to catch up with Corporal Davis. These two weeks of stand-alone leadership came with the assignment of my squad on a distant combat outpost mission. Though our battalion was in Corps reserve, way behind the front line, security remained a concern. The threat was from guerrilla units, North Korean soldiers who had been overrun in our assault north and caught behind our MLR. They were organized to some degree and operating behind our line (on our side) with hit-and-run actions.

My squad's outpost location was about a two-hour hard walk up several long ridgelines from our base camp, which was along the Soyang-Gang River near Inje. After arriving on the position and relieving the assigned squad, leadership responsibilities really hit home for me. I was in charge; I was totally responsible for everything that did or did not take place on our ridge. This responsibility included designating the locations of our defensive fighting holes, the best locations for my automatic weapons, and the location of my command position. I also had to determine our security activity, such as patrolling and the size of the patrol unit and if forward listening posts were necessary during darkness (and if so, where). I also had to register our supporting arms, artillery, and mortars on likely avenues of approach into our position; the responsibilities went on and on. But I loved this squad leader business. I called the shots, so to speak, and I exercised the Principles of Leadership to the fullest. That really paid off; my squad members were not only a team but also a family.

I liked the position and duty so well, as did my squad members (primarily because no one bothered us with personnel and rifle inspections, close-order drill in the rice paddies below, classes on tactics and military subjects, and so on), that we extended our mission on the outpost for another week. Another week of rest and relaxation with no hassle by the higher-ups. I learned much on that ridgeline about being a part of the team while leading it from the front, and I would build upon that throughout my Marine Corps career.

But the good life doesn't last forever. Our division was ordered back into the lines, and we moved forward into positions on the Punch Bowl near where we had been when relieved a month earlier. The peace talks had hit a snag and we were back in the attack and headed north. We unloaded from the six-bys (trucks) and spent the night behind our lines, our last night of rest. We would move out in the assault before daylight the next day.

Unfortunately for me, the next morning, as I led my squad forward in the black of night to the jump-off position, I stepped off into space. I had not done a reconnaissance of the route from our squad's night position to where we would join our platoon for the assault forward. We were behind the line, so I knew our movement forward would be safe enough, but I didn't allow for the total darkness. We were unable to see anything immediately in front of our faces, and of course we could not use lights. So while leading my squad, I fell maybe ten to twelve feet and hit the road (engineers had much earlier cut a dirt road through the ridgeline, which was not shown on my map), belly down with arms stretched outward to break my fall. My five-and-three-quarters-pound .30-caliber M-2 carbine came off my shoulder, where I had slung it, and smashed onto my right hand as I hit the road. The pain was tremendous, and I knew I was hurt. That ended this chapter of my leadership experience. The rest of this story is given in my memoir. Suffice it to say here that my hospitalization took many months and ended in the Naval Hospital in Bethesda, Maryland. That and my following assignment kept me out of leadership positions for several years.

My George Company situation involving tent liners, which is covered in a later chapter, was my next infantry leadership experience. Prior to that, however, I did a year as one of the sergeants of the guard in Marine Air Group 11 at Atsugi, Japan. While that duty amounted to being in charge of and responsible for junior Marines and ensuring that all did their duty in providing security for the air base, it fell a little short in leadership. The main reason I make that statement is because we were very much under higher levels of authority, platoon sergeants, the first sergeant, and the provost marshal. We sergeants of the guard didn't do anything on our own, and we never felt that we had the authority to do so. We followed the written orders and did what we were told to do.

Noncommissioned officer leadership has always been a point of pride in our Marine Corps. Our corporals and sergeants have led the way in all of our great battles. The staff noncommissioned officers have always been the bedrock of Marine leadership, the backbone of the Corps. However, at times the Marine

Corps has provided some negative influence in the leadership arena, and one of those times was during the early phases of our involvement with the ground war in Vietnam.

Due to the urgent need for more Marine infantry forces, the Corps needed more rifle platoon leaders—second lieutenants—than could be gained through the normal officer acquisition. The Marine Corps' solution was to commission, temporarily, five thousand staff noncommissioned officers. That helped the officer problem, but it seriously hurt the Corps' middle level of leadership— leadership at the unit level with Marines, where it is needed.

To compound the Corps' problem with a lack of good, on-site, middle-level leaders, the Marine Corps also received an influx of enlistees from Secretary of Defense Robert McNamara's so-called Project One Hundred Thousand. This program amounted to the Army and our Corps having to take people into our ranks with very low intelligence test scores, males who could not otherwise have served in the armed forces. These people required on-hand, constant guidance and leadership just when that level of leadership was weakened in our Corps. This situation brought on a bad time for our Marine Corps and for individual Marines because it was not safe to walk alone on any of our Marine Corps bases after dark. Murder, rape, and robbery were taking place among us, on all bases, in the late 1960s and early 1970s. Yes, the perpetrators wore the Marine uniform, but they were *not* Marines.

Upon their commissioning, the top five thousand staff noncommissioned officers were replaced with juniors who otherwise would not have been promoted because of their lack of experience and weakness in leading others. Also, sergeants with little time in the Corps were promoted in this catch-up game. Of course, that is the way it is in war time, and we have been through the routine many times, but it still hurts the force, the team. As a result of the disciplinary problems caused by the weakened middle-level leadership, the commandant of the Marine Corps directed commands to employ officers in the barracks and in the liberty places within towns to maintain order and the safety of Marines. This amounted to directing officers to perform the duties of midlevel leadership, which amounted to doing the senior sergeant's work.

It was several years before the Marine Corps recovered from the lack of so many middle-level leaders at one time. The commissions were temporary, and the earlier order clearly stated that when the needs of the Marine Corps went away, the temporary officers would be reverted to their enlisted ranks, of course with the considerations of enlisted promotion opportunities during the commissioned time served. The reversion was several years after the critical need for capable, midlevel leadership.

Most temporary officers had fifteen years or more of active-duty time when commissioned. When the reversion decision came almost four years later, the majority of the temporary officers had their twenty years in and retired. Headquarters Marine Corps also seated a board to consider and recommend deserving temporary officers for retention as regular, reserve, limited-duty, or warrant officers. Many temporary officers retired in 1970 and 1971, and quite a few were selected in the different officer categories. There were not many who were reverted to their enlisted rank because they were short on retirement years.

The Marine Corps established staff noncommissioned officer schools and academies in the late 1960s to make up for this leadership shortfall. I had paid little attention to this effort at senior sergeant education. For one thing I was very busy with my own work, but I also had never felt the need for such education. We never had senior sergeant leadership schooling when I was in the ranks; there were noncommissioned officer schools for corporals and sergeants that I wanted to experience, but I never had a chance to attend one of those. I was always put off with, "We'll do that next year when our schedule is easier and we can afford to be without you for a few weeks."

During my enlisted time, staff noncommissioned officers learned from one another, especially from senior staff noncommissioned officers. In those days we all lived in the barracks; the few married Marines in our ranks for the most part had left their wives at home. We enjoyed a 24/7 classroom environment; any issue or question was taken to a senior, who then informed you of how to handle it. We were Marines in uniform twenty-four hours a day and always together in the barracks or in the field, where we learned from one another, on the job.

Another reason for the hole or weakness in middle-level leadership at this time was the change in Marines' concept of their personal lives, meaning marriage, while in the service. By the 1970s more Marines were married and maintained a home near their unit, either on base or in the nearby town. (At this time, any Marine could get married and draw extra money for quarters and rations. In my time it was understood that one had to be a sergeant with over four years of active duty time—referred to as "E-4 over four"—to rate the government quarters and ration allowance. Otherwise, one had to have the approval of his commanding officer to receive the extra money when married.)

The major change is that married Marines have their family time. Yes, they are good Marines, but they also are good husbands and dads. They have to have family time, so this means that at some point in their day, they leave the barracks and head home. This situation got to such a point that, by the 1980s, very few Marines lived in the barracks. Even many Marines who were not married chose to live in town on their own, and they made enough money to do so. (This was not possible in my time on a sergeant's pay of $129.00 a month before taxes.) The Corps now has very few 24/7 Marines, a circumstance that contributed to the violence that took place in the early 1970s. There was no around-the-clock advice and guidance available to the young leader in the barracks. The staff noncommissioned officers who were not married lived in the base's staff non-commissioned officer quarters and away from their unit's evening happenings in the barracks. The staff noncommissioned officers' barracks also contributed to the lack of 24/7 upper-level guidance that I experienced in my time.

Initially I was not impressed with learning that Major General John I. Hudson, the director of the Education Center, Marine Corps Base, Quantico, Virginia, wanted me to be the next director of Quantico's Staff Non-Commissioned Officers Academy. The reasons I gave in the previous paragraphs contributed to my negative thoughts. Giving the issue some serious thought, however, I came to the realization that the staff noncommissioned officers' ranks had fallen short over the past few years. They needed this schooling to help them get back to the position long understood to be the backbone of the Marine Corps. I accepted the duty and really enjoyed it. The Corps needed it then, and it has it today.

I continued with my leadership approach as the director of the academy, being out and involved with my Marines. Though much of their time was spent in classrooms, and I did have my time with them there, we also got outside. Our field operations were very limited, depending on the class (each was divided by rank), but we did do the physical fitness test. As always, I ran the test with my sergeant students.

A great help to me in the academy was my sergeant major. Sergeant Major Pete Ross held that position, and he was and is my kind of a Marine. He was always out and about, involved with each class in whatever was going on, including running the physical fitness test. He was of the old school, and he was a great contributor to the progress our senior sergeants made getting back on track with the professional manner with which their ranks earlier had han-dled and led their Marines. In retirement today, Sergeant Major Ross is still very much involved in Marine activities.

Historical Traits of a Leader

To lead people, walk beside them . . .
As for the best leaders, the people do not
   notice their existence.
The next best, the people honor and praise.
The next, the people fear;
And the next, the people hate. . . .
When the best leader's work is done the
   people say,
"We did it ourselves!"

Lao-tsu

A big part of the character of those people who want to be leaders is that they have a strong desire to do just that—to influence, to motivate, and to be involved with others. There are individual traits that aid leaders, personal characteristic that followers recognize and appreciate and to which they favorably respond. When future leaders are properly motivated, they move through the learning stages of what is required for successful leadership; they study and exercise the traits of leaders. For most that motivation and desire is kindled at a young age. Young men and women entering the armed forces meet and recognize leadership from day one in boot camp or basic training. There is someone in charge of them, and that someone is responsible for getting them through the training environment and on to serving our country.

Our armed forces have been and are always involved with leadership in all respects. The traits that make a leader are taught in schools, in the field, and in the barracks. The awareness that others are involved in accomplishing the team's mission is a requirement in a military person's everyday life, and this is especially so for the leaders. Leadership is practiced by all, and those who fall short in some of the essential traits for whatever reason move on to something else, something, perhaps, on the technical side in which they can contribute and do well.

Not everyone is fit to be a leader; many fall short in too many of the required traits. Most of these people in my experience have an interest in some technical field and have the ability to do well there. They like working with their minds or their hands. This is good for our society because we cannot all do the same thing well. If we all excelled in leadership, we would be short of people in other areas and specialties. We each have our strong points and our special capabilities. Not everyone will have or be able to exercise the following fourteen traits of a leader:

- Bearing
- Integrity
- Courage (moral and physical)
- Judgment
- Decisiveness
- Justice
- Dependability
- Knowledge
- Endurance
- Loyalty
- Enthusiasm
- Tact
- Initiative
- Unselfishness

Many Marine leaders have impressed me by possessing every leadership trait listed, all fourteen of them. Corporal Davis, who is covered well in my memoir and mentioned earlier in this book, is first and foremost in this regard. Another great leader in another war possessed all of these leader traits: my battalion commander in the Vietnam War, Lieutenant Colonel George W. Smith.

I had extended my service for six months in the Vietnam War following a year of duty as an infantry battalion advisor with the Vietnamese Marine Corps, and I joined the 3rd Marine Division with further assignment to the 1st Battalion, 9th Marine Regiment. I was immediately impressed with Colonel Smith's command presence and bearing upon greeting me in his tent on Fire Support Base Ann in northern I Corps, Vietnam, in November 1968. About six feet in height, he appeared in excellent physical condition in his squared-away Marine utilities. With a warm, friendly smile, he extended his hand, saying, "Welcome aboard, Lieutenant. You are now in the best infantry battalion in I Corps, and in the Marine Corps for that matter. Have a seat and tell me about yourself."

Though I was only a first lieutenant, and Marine rifle company commanders are captains, I sincerely hoped to get command of a rifle company. Colonel Smith was the leader who could make that happen, but he wasn't about to give command of his Marines to just anybody coming along. I quickly realized that he was going to get to know me, or at least have a good feeling of where I was coming from, before he turned over a rifle company of about two hundred of his Marines.

"Sir," I replied, "I just finished a year as an advisor with a Vietnamese Marine infantry battalion and extended six months in order to serve with our Marines up here. My hope is that I can get command of a rifle company and get on with this war. I really am not impressed with the way the Vietnamese higher-ups run their war. My opinion is that it is more on the order of search and avoid rather than search and destroy. Their Marines do well in a fight; it is the higher commanders and particularly the political heads that give me the impression they didn't want the war to end until they had collected their retirement nest egg."

"Where did the Tet Offensive catch you?"

"My battalion was in the mountains in II Corps when it broke out, and we were flown back to Saigon, where we cleared the northeastern portion of the city and outlying countryside of the bad guys. We had some good fights."

"Do you have a family back home?"

"Yes, Sir, I have a dear wife and two little daughters, the youngest born one month after I got in country last year. I was just home with them on my thirty-day leave for extending my time over here."

"How did your wife take your extension of your time here for another six months?"

"It was not easy for her, Sir. We met in Hawaii on my R&R [rest and recreation] from the advisor unit, and it was there that I expressed my desire to extend my time over here. She listened to my reasoning and finally agreed through many tears. She said, 'If that is what you feel you have to do, I'll get by another six more months, somehow.' She knows and appreciates my feeling of duty to our Corps and country. She is one great lady, with an eagle-, globe-, and anchor-shaped heart, just like a Marine. My extension of duty over here may work against the thought, but we are very much in love. She is the only lady for me."

"Great, I'm married to a lady just like you described. When did you go thorough TBS [the Basic School]?"

"I never did, Sir. I'm one of those staff noncommissioned officers presented with a temporary commission in '66. The only officer schooling or training I have was taking the Basic Officer Extension Course provided by the Marine

Corps Institute. I completed that course several years ago by mail when I was a technical sergeant. No OCS or TBS, Sir."

"Well, that's no big thing. You surely have the experience and maturity required for rifle company command in combat."

We covered my past eighteen years in the Corps, which included my Korean War experience, 1st Force Reconnaissance Company and other duty assignments, and my training and personal desires along the way—and all the while with his steady look right into my eyes. I was impressed with this Marine commander, and I very much wanted to work for him in any position. Colonel Smith welcomed me aboard with the command of his Alpha Company.

Alpha Company provided the security for that fire-support base for several more days, and I really got to know my new commander. That knowledge wasn't acquired only in his command post. He got out among his Marines, and he always conversed in a friendly manner with those he met: "How is it going, Corporal? Are you getting mail from home? How do you like our chow? Do you have any problems with our mess tent, or our chow hours?"

Colonel Robert H. Barrow was our 9th Marine regimental commander. I didn't check in with my new regiment but flew directly to the fire-support base from the 3rd Marine Division Headquarters as I had been directed. However, I must have met Colonel Barrow during my bounce around in headquarters because he called Colonel Smith to tell him to expect me and recommended me strongly for consideration of command. Another thought I have at this writing, however, is that Colonel Barrow may have talked with the senior Marine advisor in Saigon by phone, referencing my transfer and the extension of my combat tour.

Colonel L. V. Corbett had told me prior to my departure from the advisor unit that he would make sure the 3rd Marine Division had a job for me. He had some contacts up there and would make a few phone calls on my behalf. At the time I didn't realize that he was going to get involved on a personal basis. What I know is that Colonel Smith, early in my assignment with him, mentioned to me several times that our regimental commander wanted me to have command of a rifle company and considered me one of his top lieutenants. I learned from that experience that it is a real motivator to have your immediate leader pass on positive comments about you from leaders higher in the chain of command.

Christmastime in 1968 found our entire battalion together at Vandegrift Combat Base, which gave all of us the opportunity to get to know our commander. Colonel Smith made that easy; he was always out among us, involved in whatever we were doing. I remember him once asking me what it was that one of my Marines had said to him upon saluting. (Marines don't salute in combat, but Vandegrift at that time was a safe distance from any enemy forces and saluting was the routine.) My initial thought was to wonder what in the world the Marine could have said, and I wondered if it was negative, but the colonel was smiling. I guess he saw the concern on my face and responded with, "Did he tell me what company he was in?"

Then I knew what the issue was: "Yes, sir, he just wanted to make sure that you knew that he was in Alpha Company, the best company out here, as he does with all officers he meets." My battalion commander responded very favorably to that approach.

Earlier, during one of my Marine talks while pushing esprit and pride of the team, I had suggested that when we saluted an officer we let him know that we are in the best company in the battalion. "Alpha One Nine, Sir" was as easy as saying, "Good Afternoon, Sir." I followed with my thought that this would show one's pride in the company. I knew my Marines were doing that with me and our platoon leaders. It really pleased me to hear my commander's positive comments on the greeting as well as his compliments on what he had observed with my company. He recognized and appreciated the fact that I was conducting tactical training classes (actually, refresher training) with my Marines while at Vandegrift. (Details on this are covered in my memoir, *Marine Rifleman.*) Our Christmas break ended and we moved back into the bush.

A month later we were all back at Vandegrift getting ready for Operation Dewey Canyon. (My company was on the operation from 20 January to 18 March 1969 as we provided firebase security for twenty days while other units moved into assault positions.) I was told to bring my platoon leaders and come up to Colonel Smith's tent for a briefing on the operation. My officers and I learned a lot that evening, and it started with "Please help yourself to a drink there on the box, soda, beer, or a mixed drink." Then we really got to know our commander. We learned what to expect from him in certain tight situations, what he expected from us, and, in short, just how we were going to conduct this upcoming operation. Colonel Smith had been a tactics instructor at the Basic School when he was a captain, and we now got the full course. There was no end to his knowledge of infantry tactics. I knew we had a winning team because our leader possessed all the necessary leader traits; he was one of us, out there with us, and a key member of the team.

Next we were in the A Shau Valley on Operation Dewey Canyon. Our commander didn't visit us by helicopter and an hour or so later return to his safe rear-area command post for a comfortable night with all of the personal conveniences and comforts—as some other services' battalion commanders conducted their war. Our commander was right out there with us, suffering and enduring the same life threats and the scarcity of water, rations, and medical needs, not to mention the loss of the comforts of life. Our colonel, his command group, and our Headquarters and Service Company were always on the ridge with us, sandwiched between Charlie Company and my Alpha. I had daily personal contact with my commander, which I greatly appreciated because we were heavily committed and involved in an unknown situation with almost daily enemy contact. His enthusiasm for our mission and objectives was contagious. The A Shau Valley was the North Vietnamese Army's personal turf; neither U.S. nor Vietnamese forces had ever been in this northern part of the valley.

A big factor working against us on this operation was the weather. We were in the monsoon season, which meant daily heavy rains, and this greatly reduced suitable flying weather. Helicopters don't fly into jungle landing zones when the pilot cannot see out of his aircraft. It stood to reason that during this time there would be many days unsuitable for chopper flights, meaning there would be no resupply of ammo, water, or rations, and worse, there would be no evacuation of our casualties. This fact was a plus in the sense that the North Vietnamese commander would never consider the possibility of U.S. forces entering the A Shau Valley. If that commander did believe the weather would hold up offensive action, he didn't allow for the United States Marines' warrior mentality. We did, and we caught him with his pants down. For the entire six weeks–plus that we were in the A Shau, the enemy forces had to play "catch-up ball." They never did get it together.

Colonel Smith was in the middle of it all with a decisive read-out of what to do next. He was personally involved in all of our company actions, such as my big battle on 22 February. He was on the ridge above me, maybe three thousand meters distance. He could not only hear the battle going on below him but also feel the concussion from the grenades, mortar rounds, and rocket-propelled grenade explosions. In spite of all of this, he never once bothered me with a radio call asking for a situation report, as some commanders did in that war. Some time into that fight, when I had a free moment, it occurred to me to call my battalion commander with an update on our situation. I knew that he was concerned, and I was glad that he had not bothered me with asking for a report earlier, when I was physically involved in the battle.

When I called, Colonel Smith, not his radio operator, answered, saying, "Delmar Six here, what's happening Hammer-hand?" As I filled him in on what had taken place, telling him that the enemy force was larger than expected, that our artillery and air the night before had completely missed the target, a rocket-propelled grenade fired at me missed but hit a bush to my immediate left rear. The explosion only two feet away showered me with shrapnel and concussion, breaking my radio contact as it knocked me to the ground. After my recovery, I called my commander again, and now he was really concerned. "Can I send some help down to you?" he asked.

Charlie Company was the closest to me, but they couldn't leave the headquarters and command group, or the two captured 155-mm field guns, which were still a concern. Delta Company had reached our ridgeline on the Laotian border, but I needed help now and they were hours away. As we discussed my situation, I realized that Delta couldn't help me with our fight, but I would surely need help in carrying out my casualties and providing security when it was over. I agreed with my colonel: Send Delta.

The story of Captain Edward Riley, Delta's company commander, and Delta Company is in a later chapter of this book. My Alpha Marines won that battle, and we returned to the top of the ridge after darkness fell. Though it was late into the night, Colonel Smith was waiting for us with congratulations on a job well done.

Colonel Smith had his own call signs, or maybe a better term would be nicknames, for his company commanders. Shortly after joining the battalion I heard him on the radio referring to Delta's Captain Riley as "Cold Steel." I really liked that name and was envious; what could be a better name for a Marine warrior? Captain John Kelly of Charlie Company was "Blackjack." Then came my nickname. We were on an operation, and I got a radio call and heard "Hammer Head." Well that really didn't fire me up or please me. Hammerhead sharks might be bad, but still . . .

I was in the colonel's command post the following day and he asked, "Wes, what do you think of your personal call sign?"

"Well, Sir, it's OK, but I don't know much about hammerheads."

"What? Hammer Head? My call sign for you is Hammer Hand." And he made a fist with his right hand and acted as though he was smashing something. "That's you! Hammer Hand!"

"I like that, Sir. I guess my radio was not receiving very well since it sounded like you said Hammer Head."

"No, no! You are the hammer of this battalion, my Hammer Hand." And I heard Hammer Hand from then on.

I have the Medal of Honor because Colonel Smith wanted me to have it for my action on 22 February 1969. My senior company corpsman, Hospitalman Second Class Charles M. Hudson initiated the action with a visit to Colonel Smith on the ridgeline a day after our fight. Doc told our commander what he had seen take place in that fight; he outlined my involvement and included just how hopeless he had felt about our chances of surviving the battle while he tended to the many wounded on the ground around him. As a result of Doc Hudson's words, Colonel Smith interviewed each of my rifle platoon sergeants (all of whom survived that fight without even a wound) and others, and had each write statements in support of his recommendation for my award.

We were on that operation for another month, one firefight after another, trying to stay alive, and through it all my commander didn't put off or lay aside his paper work. With a stubby pencil and wet paper, he did the write up for his Marines' awards; he took care of all of us. He didn't stop with the write ups and submission of his recommendations to higher headquarters. Later on, he followed the progression upward from one command to the next higher. He took care of his Marines.

Somewhere up that chain of command, however, a commander did not do Colonel Smith justice. Our regimental and division commanders wrote Lieutenant Colonel George W. Smith up for the Navy Cross for his personal involvement and actions in our many enemy force engagements on Operation Dewey Canyon, and somewhere up the chain of command, the Navy Cross recommendation was downgraded to a Silver Star, which was a major disappointment for me. Colonel Smith's actions and involvement in our daily activities against the enemy forces were most deserving of the Navy Cross. The two captured 155-mm enemy guns were just one reason why.

The "Walking Death Battalion" finally got out of the A Shau Valley, and our commander ensured that we came out together, as a team. But due to bad weather and another commitment with another friendly force, we were about ten days longer in that valley than the other two battalions of our regiment. Our battalion got through Operation Dewey Canyon as well as we did because of our courageous, dependable commander. Not only did he have all of the ideal commander's leadership traits, but he exercised them daily. We would never have made it with someone in the commander's position who was short on any one of the fourteen essential traits.

Our battalion's duties following Dewey Canyon included each rifle company being assigned a tactical area of operation in which we ran patrols looking for the bad guys. Periodically, one or more companies would be assigned a specific mission with another larger force such as a battalion; the mission for the rifle company amounted to setting up an ambush or holding force. In this operation the larger force would sweep the area, pushing the enemy into the holding force in what was known as a hammer-and-anvil operation. After Dewey Canyon my Alpha Company was on such a mission, and we had been out in the bush for several days. I received a radio call from Delmar-6 (Colonel Smith): "Hammer Hand, Bulldozer-6 [our regimental commander, Colonel Robert Barrow] is having a change of command party tomorrow evening here at Vandegrift and you are invited. Over."

I appreciated the thought but I couldn't leave my company, especially on an operation. I responded, "Delmar-6, Delmar Alpha -6. Sir, I would surely like to attend that party, but as you know, I am on an operation and can't make it. Please pass to Bulldozer-6 my appreciation for the invitation and my regrets. Over."

"Hammer Hand, there is no enemy force in your area larger than platoon size, and your executive officer can easily handle your company in your absence for one night and two days. There will be a chopper at your position around ten hundred tomorrow morning for you. You get on that chopper. You will make the party."

That ended that issue. I responded, "Roger your last. Out."

My return to Vandegrift was early enough for me to get a good shower, shave, and put on a clean set of jungle utilities. The reception and dinner were held in the Vandegrift base's officer's area, which served meals as well as club benefits in their big connected tents. My two gin and tonics during the reception worked quickly on my dehydrated, C-ration–fed body.

While I enjoyed the camaraderie and the great steak meal that followed, I couldn't get my mind off of my Marines, my team, who were not enjoying any of this and were possibly in harm's way at the moment. I worked hard at convincing myself that Colonel Smith was correct; there was no enemy force around that could hurt my Marines. Nevertheless, it was a highly emotional evening for me, and I was keenly aware of my love for this team of leaders and for my family of Marine warriors.

What really made the evening for me followed the meal. We moved back into the reception tent, and Colonel Barrow shouldered his guitar and picked and sang for us. Was there anything that this great Marine commander could not do? That was just too much, and I almost lost it. My Marine emotions were running at an extremely high level, and they continued afterward, back in my tent in Alpha Company's area. Sleep didn't come easily that night. Oh how I love Marines and the Marine Corps.

Alpha Company was in the bush when our battalion commander's change of command occurred. I missed it. Colonel Smith's following duty was as the operations officer on the staff of Task Force Hotel at Vandegrift Combat Base. I didn't see him again until my departure from Vietnam, when I sought him out to say thanks and goodbye as I passed through Vandegrift. Again, I felt guilty for leaving my Marines as they were moving back into the A Shau Valley on another operation, named Apache Snow. Giving voice to my feelings, my colonel assured me that I had already done more than my share. He told me to take off the pack, go home, and join my family. They needed me, and it was now their turn to receive my attention. He gave me his home phone number with the suggestion that I call his wife, Nan, with words from Vietnam. I did.

Colonel Smith retired from the Marines as a major general with three wars behind him, World War II, Korea, and Vietnam. He is on the list of great Marine leaders, and he has great Marines following in his footsteps. His sons are Marines, too. George is currently the commanding officer of our Basic School in Quantico and Andrew is the commanding officer of Marine Barracks, 8th and I Street, Washington, D.C. What do his sons' assignments say about the dad? Leadership. They have all of these leadership traits, and one, if not both, will be a future commandant of the Marine Corps.

All Marine leaders are taught the fourteen traits of a leader and are expected to live and work by them, but some exercise the traits in a personal and natural manner, as did Colonel Smith. I have outlined commonsense thoughts on the traits a person desiring to be a leader should possess and exercise. These traits are what we all want and expect from those in positions over us. Good leaders will evaluate themselves concerning each of these traits: How do I stack up? Do I fall within the positive arena of each of these traits? If not, what can I do about it?

In the next section I discuss the six essential elements of leadership. If a leader falls short in one or more of the principles of leadership, he or she can work hard to make up for it and impress others with his or her ability to lead. But a leader who lacks one of the six essential elements is not going to go very far in leading others.

SECTION II

The Essential Elements of Leadership

Care

6

A leader is a person who has the ability to get others
to do what they don't want to do, and like it.

President Harry S. Truman

C are is a personal commitment to people and to the things those people
value. A leader must care enough to commit him or herself in many
ways, but certainly to those whom he or she leads—the followers—
and to his or her mission. The exercise of care starts with the individual, who
should exhibit all of the leadership traits outlined in chapter 5.

Care for one's followers is in my opinion the number one essential element
of leadership. I have emphasized the importance of care in each chapter of this
book. When followers realize that their leader doesn't really care about them,
he is no longer their leader. He is only a figurehead. There are many ways a
leader can send a message of concern, as I have outlined in my Corporal Davis
stories, but it generally is more with actions than words. In my world leadership simply means care. Though I was aware of the meaning of that word
through the relationship and love of my parents, it really hit home for me in
the Korean War.

Is care for your followers as I describe here oxymoronic in reference to our
Marine Corps leadership in combat? If care of his Marines is so important to
the leader, and Marine leaders are known for the care of their men, how do
they handle the task of sending them forward into battle knowing that some are
going to lose limbs or, worse, their lives? That thought is always foremost in a
combat leader's mind, and there is no easy answer as to how to handle it. Some
combat leaders have not handled this issue as well as others, and I suppose
it has to do with the individual and his ability to handle stressful situations.
We all have different approaches to difficult and especially life-threatening
circumstances. The issue deserves discussion; we will break it apart and look
closely at it.

My approach has always been to recognize and accept the fact that a Marine's duty is to fight his country's battles; that is what he signed up for, and he has been thoroughly trained for it. The profession of arms and one's military obligation demand a commitment to duty. And duty within our armed forces, especially within infantry units during time of war, includes the possibility of the loss of lives while fulfilling that commitment. Our Marine warriors do not accept the fact that they will die for their country, though that possibility is recognized as a reality. Rather, our gunfighters' purpose, as General George S. Patton stated so well, is "to make that other poor SOB die for his country." Infantry Marines take on the enemies of our country and our way of life. That is their job, and they know the possible cost. The news media likes to write of their loss in combat using the phrase "gave their lives." None of those with whom I served would accept those words; they didn't give their lives, they lost them in defense of our country, our freedom, and our way of life. They lost their lives in the performance of their duty.

Commanders know that some of their men are going to pay for doing their duty with serious wounds and loss of life. However, my experience has been that Marines by nature are of the optimistic breed: "The worst is not going to happen to me and that includes my buddies, my unit, and my team." Marine leaders at all levels are always involved with and directly committed to their unit. They know what is happening, are personally concerned with the situation, and are fully involved in the solution. And that is why and how it works. Myron Davis, Bill Christman, Lee Roy Herron, Edward Riley, and George Smith, leaders of whom I write in this book, are several examples of the many Marine leaders who were personally involved with the day-to-day control and care of their Marines.

In their book *Military Leadership,* Robert Taylor and William Rosenbach examine the negative results of a leaders's failure to commit to the care and concern of his followers: "Military history is littered with the names of great and good men who were not quite hard enough, and whose disinclination to get their men killed caused only more suffering in the long run; consider again McClellen's solicitousness for his men, which may well have prolonged the Civil War by years, or Ivan Hamilton's reluctance to interfere with his subordinate commanders at Gallipoli, which threw away a campaign that might well have been won on the first day. Some writers maintain that one of the few deficiencies of Sir Harold Alexander as a field commander was his preference for the soft word, and it may have cost him the capture of most of the

German army south of Rome in May 1944. Napoleon summed it up when he sent Brune down to clean up the Vendee in 1800; he told his general it was better to kill ten thousand now than to be too soft and have to kill a hundred thousand later on."

Then there is the later-occurring personal side of this stressful issue, the after-effect that appears to bother some men later in life: post-traumatic stress disorder (PTSD). I will address this issue in detail in chapter 9, but my thoughts on PTSD are along the lines of the individual and his contribution to or the lack thereof to the team effort. War is ugly; war is hell. But we Americans enjoy our lives within our free society because our men have gone to war and did what had to be done. They were trained to fight that war, and that fight included the realization that humans would be maimed for life and others would die in battle.

Leadership includes stepping forward and doing what ought to be done, regardless of the personal displeasures and difficulties that might accompany that effort. Just because that is the way it is, and the way it has always been done, doesn't mean a leader should accept it as the way he will tackle it when he takes into consideration the care of his followers. A leader must ask himself what is in the best interest of his followers—and their best interest includes a wide range of issues, not just combat.

I do not hear well today; my reception of higher-frequency sounds is gone. How does this tie in with leadership responsibility and care? Weapons fire was the cause of my hearing loss. A firefight in combat doesn't help ones' hearing for sure, but that situation usually is not drawn out over time. It is the hour after hour, day after day of loud, destructive noise that causes major damage to one's hearing. The problem was in boot camp and throughout the Marine Corps rifle and pistol ranges in the 1950s, when we fired weapons for hours and days at a time.

The damage was done because I did not use ear covering or any kind of hearing protection. A shooters has bare ears not only to his own rifle and pistol fire but also to that of the Marines on both sides of him, six to eight feet away. I would come off the firing line and not hear a word spoken to me in a normal voice. I do not know upper-level leadership's involvement with this situation at the time, but for sure they—someone—should have known what was going on and provided some corrective action. They, the leaders at all levels, were responsible and should have shown some care for their young Marines.

My boot camp experience (which was the same for all Marine recruits, and that routine continued up through the years) included the word that corpsmen had cotton that we could stuff in our ears, "if needed." That information in boot camp was provided in such a negative manner—and with the added phrase "If any of you girls need it"—that none of us went to the corpsman. My rifle fire (from a .30-caliber, M-1 rifle, semiautomatic) was bad enough, but the rifles on each side of me were just as loud and damaging to my hearing. And the noise didn't stop on the rifle range. There was the pistol range with very loud .45-caliber pistols exploding at six feet on each side of you, and that pistol did more damage to the ears than the rifle fire. The Browning automatic rifle and machine-gun fire, and of course the hand-grenade explosions on that range, were also part of the package. None of us were girls, therefore, none of us hear very well today. Who should have cared and who was responsible?

As the platoon sergeant of 2nd Platoon, George Company, 3rd Battalion, 5th Marine Regiment, 1st Marine Division in Korea in October 1954, I had an opportunity to provide and take special care of my Marines. I wanted to do for my Marines in a manner that they could appreciate, that would make their daily lives more enjoyable during the coming winter. The fighting of that war had ceased, though tensions were still very high and we were ready to handle any combat situation that might arise. That included manning defensive positions on the United Nations' MLR, located on the ridgeline known as Baker Block. Rather than live on the actual defensive line, we were set up at the base of the ridge on the south side and lived in tents.

Combat infantry Marines living in tents? Boy, I thought, this Marine life is really getting easy. I had just reported in for duty, and as a buck sergeant (pay grade E-4 then) I was pleased to get a staff sergeant's job as one of the company's three rifle platoon sergeants. We did live in tents with a squad of thirteen Marines to a tent. But that was the best that could be said about our living conditions. The tents had two kerosene stoves, one at each end, but the air flow through the tent was such that little heat was felt on those cold winter nights. A Marine two sleeping cots from a stove had no benefit of heat from the stove.

I had learned during my prior tour of duty in Japan that there were cloth tent liners available that really improved the tent life. Not only did their white color improve the inside appearance in both brightness and atmosphere, but they greatly reduced the air flow from the outside and helped retain the heat from the small kerosene stoves. I approached our company first sergeant and inquired about tent liners only to learn that they were not available in the 1st Marine Division. "Yes, some rear echelon Marines might have them back at division headquarters, but we can't get them up here."

Well, that answer wasn't good enough. I thought I could get tent liners from the Army. The Army always had plenty of everything. With the first sergeant's jeep and several visits to nearby Army units, I came up with tent liners. These had been used and were in this Army unit's discard bin, but they were tent liners and would serve my purpose. My Marines loved them, and the action immediately removed me from the "New Guy" list to "My Platoon Sergeant." My 2nd Platoon Marines were the only ones with tent liners, and the rest of George Company focused on the fact that the 2nd Platoon's sergeant took care of his Marines. They wondered why they couldn't also have tent liners.

As a platoon sergeant I lived in a small four-man tent, and I didn't bother with getting a liner for it. We were in it only for sleeping, and the liner wouldn't have done much for us. Our stove was in the center of the tent and our racks were close to it. I didn't even ask the Army if a liner was available. One of my Marines did comment on the fact that I didn't get one for myself. "Why?" he asked.

A five-day field operation up on our defensive line that started the following day, plus the word that we were returning to the States within a couple of months, took the heat off my fellow platoon sergeants. But they really caught it for several days: "The 2nd Platoon sergeant cares for and provides for his Marines."

My regiment, the 5th Marines, returned from Korea to Camp Pendleton, California, in 1955 and set up in Camp San Margarita. The barracks were nice, clean, and squared away compared to the tents in which we had lived in Korea. In those days Marines lived in what was known as "squad bays" within the barracks, which were large, open areas with sleeping racks down both sides. (I never learned why they were called squad bays because they handled a platoon—or three squads, about fifty men.) The head (toilets, wash sinks, and showers) included two small rooms off from the center of the building with the squad bays on each end from the head. The showers were in one room, and the commodes, urinals, and wash sinks shared another narrow room.

The sinks lined one side of the room, and the commodes and urinals were down the other side. The room was about twelve feet wide, giving about eight feet between a commode and a sink. The problem was that you could be brushing your teeth while close behind you another Marine was blowing out a commode. That problem was compounded by the odor, because Marines tended not to flush the commode right away, if ever. True, that is the way the Marine Corps had the commodes arranged, and that was the expected use of the facilities. There is no scheduled time for emptying one's bowels, after all; one has to go when the urge hits.

After a while I became incensed with the fact that many young Marines (unaware, of course) sat on the commode as though they wanted to hatch it. Again, this went on daily with little or no regard for those using the sinks directly in front of them, shaving and brushing their teeth. As one of the company's platoon sergeants, I decided to do something about it, at least with my platoon members. At an evening formation I brought up the subject to my 2nd Platoon members. As I started into my talk, I was surprised and pleased to hear the platoon sergeant of the 3rd Platoon on our left, Sergeant Shelton Lee Eakin, direct his Marines to listen up and pay heed to what Sergeant Fox was saying. The problem I was addressing was not news to any Marine because we all lived with the same issue and all wanted the same thing: a better way to lead our daily lives.

Though everyone was offended by the routine, no one had approached or even presented the issue. No one had asked what we could do about it. Now here it was. I laid out before my Marines a recommendation for a better way of life in the head. "Don't hatch it!" I said. "You drop it, flush it down the drain, right then! We have plenty of water, and your buddy brushing his teeth in front of you doesn't need the odor." I also blasted those who left without flushing the commode: "Be considerate of the other person, your buddy Marine." It worked. The morning routine in the head improved for all of us, believe it or not. We cared.

When a leader cares for his followers, he will be involved with them, and this involvement is not a "pick and choose" matter. A real leader takes on the difficult, the undesirable, and the dangerous tasks facing him and his followers as well as the pleasurable affairs. If it is a fun event, one that doesn't come around often, and all look forward to the occasion, the leader can be excused for missing it. It is during the tough events, the ones that no one wants to deal with, that the leader must be on the scene, no excuse acceptable. I experienced this situation in 1st Force Reconnaissance Company at Camp Pendleton, California, in 1961.

Our Pathfinder Platoon was scheduled for some prisoner of war experience, and I suppose this could be considered training. The first big problem, however, was that none of us knew anything about it or that it was about to take place, absolutely nothing, from me, the platoon sergeant, on down to the lowest snuffie. We were scheduled for a Monday night parachute operation; that didn't happen because the jump aircraft from El Toro never arrived at the Camp Pendleton air field. (I won't go into all of the difficult happenings that took place, from the cancelled jump to our arrival at the prisoner of war compound miles away from Camp Pendleton, because this is covered in detail in my memoir.) Unknown to us, the plan had been to put us out of the plane, two jumpers at a time, and a rifle company (nearly two hundred Marines) on the drop zone was supposed to grab each jumper as he hit the ground, tie him up, and place him in a covered truck bed.

We instead arrived by truck at the prisoner of war compound in the middle of the night. We had no idea where we were or what was about to take place. We would later learn that this compound was Warner Springs, the Navy's Air Survival, Evasion, Resistance, and Escape training school in the mountains about forty-five miles east of Camp Pendleton. And it was literally all uphill from there—over huge boulders.

The important point is our impression of our leader's lack of care, which was expressed by his non-involvement with us in the misery and torture that we, the members of his team, his followers, endured. Yes, he cared enough to give us the prisoner of war training, and it was realistic enough, but he should have been with us or completely out of the picture. We should not have seen him on the other side of the fence, period. Our platoon leader was First Lieutenant Patrick Duffy, and while my story here will not paint a good picture of him, we became close friends. We later deployed with our Pathfinder Team 44 to Okinawa; he was the team leader, and I was the assistant team leader. In our fifteen months together over there, the Warner Springs incident never came up between us. He obviously recognized his mistake in being on the opposite side of the fence from his Pathfinders. He was later killed while serving as an infantry major in the Vietnam War.

Lieutenant Duffy was the only officer in the Pathfinder Platoon at this time (two of our lieutenants were away at jump school in Fort Benning, Georgia), but I do not believe that rank was the issue. A better way for Lieutenant Duffy to have set up the training event would have been to have some other officer cover his role of supervisor in the exercise. The commander of the rifle company handling us, or one of our recon company officers, easily could have filled the bill.

Lieutenant Duffy was not with us as a prisoner; he was around, but he wasn't going through the prisoner hassle, the strip and search, the interrogations, and the torture boxes. He wasn't being thrown into the heavily fenced compound. Worse, he seemed to be in charge and directing the activity taking place because he was always in the building where the interrogations were conducted. He refused to look at me as I was escorted in and out of that building. If he had, I would no doubt have been in trouble with my senior because of the disrespectful look I had ready for him. I deeply resented his not being with us, on our side.

We spent four days in that compound, experiencing the many torture boxes, the interrogations, the lack of sufficient food, water, and no sleeping gear on that cold mountain at night. (Our utility jackets [shirts] were even taken from us, leaving us with only a skivvie shirt.) Our lieutenant was always there, but he wasn't with us, and that hurt. And I wasn't the only platoon member who resented the lieutenant not being a part of the team. Upon seeing the lieutenant through the compound fence on several occasions, a number of Marines sounded off with negative comments.

If, for whatever reason, Lieutenant Duffy didn't need or want the compound training, he should have gone home. He should have gotten lost. Maybe he thought he was giving me a leadership opportunity by being the senior Marine in the compound. If so, thanks, but my lieutenant should never be on the other side of the fence from me. He added to my confusion and misery. (My rank was technical sergeant, E-6, and actually the Marine Corps had just changed the name of my stripes to "acting gunnery sergeant" until selected for gunnery sergeant, E-7. With a three-letter name I had to write a twenty-one-letter rank before it.) I actually felt hatred toward my lieutenant at the time, a feeling probably compounded by the pain I suffered in those many and varied torture boxes.

We learned from the rifle company Marines that the training would end on Friday morning. That information came about due to our rough relationship with these rifle company Marines, who earlier had not talked with us except to try to use some foreign language to us or in our presence. My recon Marines, nevertheless, were communicating through the fence and during the torture experiences in the boxes with comments such as "You SOB, just wait until I meet you on the street in Oceanside, your ass is gonna be mine." There was enough of that attitude expressed by my Pathfinders that as early as Thursday evening, the infantry Marines were talking with us as Marines, not as the enemy. They had an interest in bettering our attitude toward them.

On Friday, around midmorning, we Pathfinders were all standing around in a group in the compound expecting the word that our misery was over. Lieutenant Duffy walked out of the headquarters shack, approached the compound fence, and stated, "Gunny, fall the platoon in."

"Whose side are you on now, Lieutenant?" I spouted off without much thought other than my resentment that our leader was with the bad guys, on the other side of the fence from us. That response didn't come across well at the receiving end.

"Damn it, Gunnery Sergeant, I said fall the platoon in, *now!*" His explosion got my Marine mind back in working order. I fell the platoon in, and our lieutenant told us that the experience was over. He followed with some positive comments of what we had accomplished, but all we heard was that it was over. Now it appeared that our leader cared enough about us to join our ranks again.

Leader care was missing in this training event. Our leader had chosen to not share our misery with us; worse, he appeared to add to it. Yes, we learned a lot on the prisoner of war side, but many of us became aware of a major negative factor in leadership. A leader has to care enough to suffer the tough times with his team members.

I write in chapter 10 about Army rifle company officers living in tents on the reverse side of the defended ridge or MLR in the Korean War. This position was behind their rifle platoons deployed on the forward slope. How does this separation from any possible ground action by the enemy fit with the concept of care for those leaders' riflemen, their followers? Care for self comes across loud and clear, and it is no wonder that the term "bug out" was so well known and used by the members of that service in the Korean War.

If the message a leader gives is that he cares only for himself, there is no team because there are no followers. Care means involvement, commitment. The only way a platoon commander on the reverse slope would know of what was happening within his squads in the situation described above was by radio, and our radios at that time were not a positive means of communication. Sometimes they worked, sometimes they didn't. I guess that was true also of that kind of leadership: Sometimes it worked, sometimes it didn't.

In 1973 and 1974, as the executive officer of Marine Security Guard, Company Alpha located in Frankfurt, Germany, my primary duty was to inspect the twenty-eight Marine detachments in all of our embassies located in capitals from Rome, Italy, north to Oslo, Norway, and from Reykjavik, Iceland, east to Moscow, Russia. The inspection included administering the physical fitness test to the Marines, and I chose to take the fitness test with them. Because the Marines on duty could not be tested with the main group, with each detachment a second test was given on the day following the first test. I was both conducting and personally running our physical fitness test about every day and loved it. I was in top physical shape. However, my primary purpose in being physically involved was to impress my Marines with the fact that I was a member of the team, the family, and that I cared about them.

How did I give the test and run it at the same time? Initially several of my Marines voiced their concern regarding this issue: "If you are running with us, Captain, how will you know what our time is on the run?" Voiced too was the concern that when the faster runners completed their three-mile run, no one would be at the finish line to record their run time. After all, I was a forty-two-year-old captain laying out my plan for the test, and it was assumed I would be somewhere back on the run trail.

My answer was simply, "If you come in ahead of me, you get credit for an eighteen-minute run, a hundred points." That brought some chuckles, like "this will be an easy test." But I was running the three miles in just over eighteen minutes, and anyone ahead of me deserved the full credit. I even got my run time down below eighteen minutes during that time, but no one gained more than ten to twenty seconds on their run time for a couple extra points.

A problem with giving the test and running it at the same time was the fact that I liked a warm-up run before the timed run. I learned to handle that by giving all participants a ten-minute break following the pull-up and sit-up tests. My guidance was that we would start the run on my command in ten minutes, and they were to be on line and ready. I did my warm-up run, approached the start point as planned, and still fifty yards or so from the start line, I would make an obvious start of my stopwatch with hand movements as I yelled, "Go." I was ready for the run; the younger guys had to warm up on the watch's time. "Move over New Corps, Old Corps coming through!" Very few Marines got to the finish line before me that first year, but they were ready for me the next time around.

The commanding officer of the 1st Battalion, 6th Marines was always involved with his Marines during my assignment in that position. This was in 1983, and at that time most Marine battalions had a high rate of disciplinary problems, especially those on deployment and away from their families and home life. Misuse of alcohol was a biggie, as well as fights, misbehaving with a local female, and absence without leave in the little Okinawa towns. And these were regular occurrences. My hope and plan was to have none of that within our battalion; we would have no disciplinary issues while deployed on Okinawa. I wanted One-Six to be the best battalion on the island. My Marines wanted the same, if they thought about it. I gathered the battalion in the base theater and addressed "care."

My approach was along the lines of, "We are here for six months. How are we going to use this time? What can we gain from it? Do we sit on this rock for the entire time or go off and do some interesting operations? Periodically, one or more battalions of this division will be deployed to Korea, Japan, and other islands on operations as well as deployed aboard naval ships as a contingency force. The commanding general will assign his best battalions to these operations, and if we are the best, we don't sit on this rock."

I continued with my main point: "Marines are noted for taking care of each other in combat. We never leave a fallen Marine behind. When we come out from a firefight, we all come out. Why does this taking care of each other, supporting your buddy Marine, happen only in combat? When your buddy needs help, give it to him, whenever and wherever. What I'm talking about, Marines, are the disciplinary problems that other infantry battalions have on this island. Alcohol, fighting, trouble out in town, failure to report in, and abuse of local women. You and I don't want any of that in our battalion because One-Six is the best battalion here. We know that; the commanding general will learn that fact.

"How do we do it? We all have our weak moments with periods of frustration and indiscretion. But we also have each other, Marines taking care of Marines. What I am talking about, Marines, is that you, each of you, are responsible for your buddy. If he is about to drink too much alcohol, get him back to the barracks. If he is about to do something that will get him in trouble, get him in a cab and barracks bound. You are responsible for each other, not just in a firefight but 24/7, wherever we are.

"Another thought, if any one of you, at any time, for whatever reason, feel that you have to consume a lot of alcohol, get drunk, then do it in the barracks where we can take care of you. Though it is against the Marine Corps and base regulations and policy, I will assume the responsibility for the act. You are that important to me and to our team. If you have to do it, do it here. Remember, Marines take care of each other, and not only in combat."

Our deployment went forward without one disciplinary problem coming to my attention. The reason was that my Marines wanted it that way. Eighteen- to twenty-year-old young men have much ahead of them to experience, and that is part of the problem. They want to get it on, to be able to say, "I've been there, done that." The team, however, means much more to them, especially when it is a Marine team with an objective that each individual considers his personal objective. My Marines took care of each other and that enabled our battalion to accomplish our objective.

Years later at Officer Candidates School, I continued with my personal involvement and enjoyed the sweaty endeavors. My sergeant major, Alford L. McMichael, and I didn't miss any activity involving our candidates, their field tests, their runs, their humps, or their physical fitness tests. At the OCS stage in my life I was no longer maxing the Marine Corps physical fitness test due to my reduced run time, but I was out there sweating with my candidates and their company leaders giving the "I care" message. This was my last leadership position in our Marine Corps, and the commanding general even gave me an extra year in the position. Thank you, Sir!

Most officers go to OCS for up to ten weeks at the beginning of their Marine Corps time. I didn't do it that way; I didn't go there for my commission. When I did go to the Marine Corps' OCS, at the end of my Marine career, it took me 156 weeks—three years—to get through it. And I loved it.

Personality

7

Leaders are made, not born. Leadership is forged in times of crisis. It's easy to sit there with your feet up on the desk and talk theory. Or send someone else's kids off to war when you've never seen a battlefield yourself. It's another thing to lead when your world comes tumbling down.

Lee Iacocca, Where Have All the Leaders Gone?

Although Lee Iacocca writes that leaders are made, not born, there are those who feel that leaders are born, not made. Adolf von Schell, the German World War I captain I quoted in my introductory chapter, states in his book *Battle Leadership* that leaders are born. Those of the born-leader school of thought are generally from the nineteenth century and earlier, including those who believe that certain people—kings, for example—are leaders due to their birthright. While birthright is no longer recognized as a means of producing leaders within our society, there are many people born with a leader personality. I refer to those who have the personal characteristics that suit leadership, and that leader position is helped if they know and exercise the leader traits.

I believe we get leaders who are both born and made. The deciding factor is the desire of the individual. If you really want to be a leader, study the traits that make a leader along with the principles of leadership, and observe the positive influences of those who are leaders, you can be one. People's personalities come to them with their birth for the most part, but childhood environment has a big influence on how they later see their role in life, how they get along with others, and whether or not they want to please or at least be on the positive side of those with whom they are involved. Some don't handle a tough childhood life as well as others, and this influences personalities and can rub off negatively in later people-to-people relationships.

Another negative influence on some future personalities is the lies parents tell their small children. Parents teach their children to be truthful, to not lie, but most children at about the age of eight learn that there is no Santa Claus, no Easter Bunny. They also learn that the stork didn't bring their little sister to them from heaven. Doesn't this amount to lies to our children? Is this approach, provided for the fun and enjoyment of our children, worth the later consequences? Could these parental games be a hole in the building of the personal integrity of our future citizens? (Are some untruths not lies and therefore acceptable?) While I accepted the Santa Claus revelation well enough and continued the game with my younger siblings and my own children, I know of individuals who were very much bothered by the facts upon leaning the truth. One close friend was so bothered when he learned the truth that it took him quite a while to get over the lie. He did not raise his son with a belief in Santa Claus.

A personality characteristic that makes a born leader is charisma. Those leaders with charisma are ahead of the game from the start because they appeal to people. Like Hollywood stars, they catch the eye and collect followers. On the other hand, a person without charisma who desires to be a leader can be a leader and a good one. He may well have to work at it a little harder; he will have to help his followers learn that he is a friend and that he cares about them. His personal involvement with his team is his path and direction into the position of leading his team members.

Followers, especially young people, who truly respect and like their leader have positive ways of expressing their devotion to that leader. Two situations during my drill instructor days in Marine Corps boot camp illustrate this point.

A 2nd Battalion drill instructor at San Diego Marine Corps Recruit Depot had a slight limp in his walk due to a leg wound he received in the Korean War. It was amazing to me to watch his platoons pass in review for their graduation parade: Each recruit, now Marines, had that same slight limp in their steps as they marched before us. He was that kind of a leader; his recruits, his followers, all wanted to be just like him.

I experienced something similar involving recruits in several of my platoons when I was asked how one could get gold in his teeth. I had received a bridge that replaced two teeth on my left side, upper row, and the bridge was fastened to the second tooth left of my front teeth. This was done with a narrow strip of gold down one side of that tooth that was visible when I talked. During their last week of training, when the heavy stuff was over, I was asked, "Can I get gold in my teeth from the Navy dentist?" These three recruits were in different platoons at different times, and one was my "house mouse," the recruit who did the house-keeping work in my duty hut, which included making up my bunk or rack. While I personally regretted having to have that bridge, others wanted to look like me. Followers will copy their leader as a son copies his father—if he is a good one.

Just because a person has charisma, however, doesn't make him or her a leader. We have seen that within our political arena time and again. Because of the charismatic way a politician presents himself to people to get their votes, for example, he receives the keys to the office he sought. Then we learn that what we couldn't see, the inside of this man's mind, the real person, was not in the best interest of the country. His thoughts were all of self; he was one of those me-first leaders concerning money, sex, power, and whatever. Our society has many wanna-be leaders who talk a great talk but can't walk the walk. Lieutenant Colonel Robert Patterson, USAF (Ret.), covered this point well in reference to his subject, Bill Clinton, in his *New York Times* bestseller, *Dereliction of Duty*.

One must have good character, solid principles, and high ethical standards in order to inspire others to follow. The major issue when recognizing a particular leader is the person under the surface; who is he, and what does he stand for? Is he loaded with the fourteen traits of a leader or is he short in one or more? If so, what are his weak traits? What are the strong points in his personality? As two old sayings have it, "Is he a person that you would want to ride the river with?" and "Can you take his word to the bank?"

Personal integrity is important to all of us, but a leader short on or without it is not a leader. If his people cannot believe in him, cannot trust him, then they are not about to follow him—certainly when the going gets rough. He that is short on integrity does not have followers; all recognize his shortcoming and realize that they will not go very far with him at the helm. Yes, there might be people in his ranks, but once they learn of his lack of integrity, he is no longer their leader, at least their effective leader.

The only character or personality trait that I would rate over integrity is courage. Courage is very important to the individual and the team because it helps us accomplish our difficult objectives. I rate courage higher than integrity simply because without courage, one can fall short in his integrity. Without the courage to hold to the line of truth, one will lie. Short on courage, one may take the easier way out of a difficult situation even if it is not the honest way or in the best interest of the team. Courage helps us hold to our basic beliefs and values: It is not mine, I will not take it; this won't be easy, but it is the right thing to do.

A leader must always be above reproach. No question is allowed concerning his integrity, his ethical standards, or his principles. Leaders are always in a fishbowl environment, always under scrutiny, and well that they should be. Visibility is what leadership is all about, out front, leading the way. A leader is a role model: "Do as I do."

Leaders must strive to reduce the gray area that has worked itself in between what is right and what is wrong in our society today. While he helps his subordinates become aware that "almost right" is not a goal, or even good enough, the leader must always operate and perform with the understanding that there is no gray between right and wrong. Integrity is a required character trait in leaders; it is a very positive trait, and the bottom line is that a person either has it or he doesn't. Can it be said of anyone that he has *some* integrity? I have stated it before and it fits here: One must have good character, solid principles, and high ethical standards to inspire others to follow.

Concerning the above statement, young Marines in the 1950s had some adjustments, maybe an awakening, as to what was right and wrong in their daily lives. From boot camp on, I understood that a Marine never lost anything. You lose something, you replace it. Usually, the source of replacement was the Marine Corps supply, the warehouse, or wherever you could get it. Though I never saw it in print, I heard noncommissioned officers from my drill instructor on repeat the phrase "A Marine never loses anything."

An example of this "midnight supply" happened during my time in boot camp. My Recruit Platoon 88 was at the rifle range, and we had just completed firing our prequalification course with the M-1 rifle. It had been a long day. We returned to our Quonset huts to find our personal gear dumped on the deck and our locker boxes (also known as foot lockers) missing. It turned out that a recruit platoon had arrived at the rifle range to find no foot lockers in their huts. No problem, go get some.

None of our personal gear was taken. My wallet, for instance, lay on the floor where it fell when my box was dumped. (We didn't use padlocks in those days; you could trust your buddy.) We got our boxes back, but the recruit platoon's action was the general mentality of small-level unit leadership then. The Marine Corps didn't have much in those days, but it would have had more in the supply racks if leadership had taken a different approach to equipment and material accountability.

Another major difference in personal property security in the 1950s (across the Marine Corps, not just in boot camp) and later years was that we didn't have to put our belongings under lock and key. (I recognize that this is contrary to my point above of midnight supply, but the help-yourself mentality was never against fellow members of the team, though it was probably behind our later need of the padlock.) After boot camp I was assigned to Baker Company, 1st Battalion, 2nd Marine Regiment, 2nd Marine Division at Camp Lejeune, North Carolina. Our Marine Corps weapons, our M-1 rifles and Browning automatic rifles, were kept in rifle racks in the center of our squad bays, as they were in boot camp. Our rifles were placed in the stands; we did not lock them. During the day there was no watch on duty to secure the rifles in the squad bay when we were in a classroom or otherwise involved without our weapons. The barracks doors were never locked. There was a fire watch on duty at night, but that was for our security against fire, not protection of the weapons.

The mentality was that Marines wouldn't take something belonging to another Marine, but Marine Corps gear, except rifles, belonged to all of us. Weapons were different, we understood that if one came up missing, the Federal Bureau of Investigation would get it back and the thief would be on his way to the stockade at Leavenworth. Later, when I returned from Korea, rifles in the racks had to be secured with a bicycle padlock. Several years after that, they had to be locked in our personal wall lockers. For years now, all weapons have been secured in the unit's armory. I suppose that is a statement about the integrity of our society as a whole. We have come a long way downward.

My Korean War experience provided another example of take what you need, though it was not in the order of midnight supply. As my Item Company moved forward to the front line for an assault in a new area, if we passed through an Army unit that we were relieving or replacing, we helped ourselves to anything we needed or wanted. Some Marines replaced their M-1 rifles with Browning automatic rifles. This was just for the assault, for the desire for more firepower. Because the automatic rifles were heavy, they would be replaced with another M-1 in the next Army unit we moved through or near following our assault. The soldiers didn't care; not one ever said anything about taking their gear. Why should they? It was easily replaced. They had plenty of everything, always.

The way our upper-level military leadership handled the Vietnam War played against most infantry commanders' beliefs and thoughts on personal integrity. Body count was the culprit. In infantry firefights and battles it was easy enough to give an accounting of the enemy's loss because after the fight, one could walk through and count the bodies as we collected their weapons and ammo for destruction. The problem was with the use of supporting arms against enemy forces located nearby.

I would have a sighting or physical contact, call in artillery and/or air support, and they would blast the area I had given them as the target. Depending upon my mission and my situation, I was not always available or free to move through the target area for a body count. It didn't matter; the officer on the other end of the radio demanded a body count. He had to show in his records the payoff for all of the ordnance used. "How many do you think were killed?" he would ask. "How many were seen that caused you to call for support in the first place? Give me a number."

What does the commander do, lie? This demand for a body count was the big reason the reported enemy number killed in action was so far off the real number. Hanoi must have wondered. I was a lieutenant at the time, and usually the voice on the radio identified himself with a senior rank—captain or major. "What is your answer?" the senior officer would ask. I would give him the number of enemy that had been observed earlier, always adding, "This is a guess. I haven't seen any bodies."

A leader must be the disciplinarian. Discipline in its true sense should never be neglected, and while enforcing it, a leader must always be kind, humane, and just. Some personalities don't fit well with handling discipline, and that is a shortfall in positive leadership. A leader praises in public and disciplines in private. Effective leaders never look the other way when infractions of rules or regulations occur. The suspected subordinate is confronted, allowed to speak in his defense, and then handled as deserved. Depending upon the severity of the offense and the subordinate's prior record, he doesn't have to be hammered. The important point is that all followers are aware that rules and regulations are to be obeyed to the letter.

I believe our society today is too lenient in providing payback for wrongs committed. In most of our society's worst cases, the culprit or offender makes out for the rest of his life. He has an easy routine of lying around every day while being provided with full, tasty meals and a dry, air-conditioned place to sleep. He has no worry about tomorrow; it is taken care of for him. And all of this easy life is of course provided at the taxpayer's expense, on the backs of the people who have to work every day. Something is not right with that picture. True, the prisoner cannot come and go as he chooses, but is that loss enough? I believe in an eye for an eye and a tooth for a tooth.

When it comes to personalities, I had a winner with my executive officer in the 1st Battalion, 6th Marine Regiment, 2nd Marine Division at Camp Lejeune. Major Earnest A. Van Huss reported for the job, and while he was a little short in the "lean and mean" visual image of the ideal Marine leader, our initial conversation impressed me with the fact that I wanted to work with him. He was very knowledgeable in all Marine matters we discussed: deployments, training, weapons, and equipment. He had just completed a tour of duty at Headquarters Marine Corps in Washington, D.C., and was now ready for some real Marine work. We would become close friends over the next year or so.

The first thing that impressed me with Ernie, in addition to his depth of knowledge of Marine matters, was his "stick-with-it" personality. At the point he joined us, I was deeply involved in getting my battalion of Marines in foot-movement condition. For infantry Marines, that means humping (walking, foot marches) because even in current times, with all of our modern means of transportation, walking is the only assured way of getting the force to where it needs to be when it needs to be there. The negative reasons for going on foot include bad weather (meaning no flying of helicopters), no transportation of any type available, and rough terrain without any roads. In my experience, Marines have faced this latter factor many times, but Marines will get it done.

At this time we were doing fast twelve- to fifteen-mile humps at about four miles per hour with all of our combat weapons and gear. My hump manner included a short (maybe a quarter of a mile), slow run about every half hour. These naturally were slow runs because of our loads, but I had learned years earlier that the break in the walk pace with the run helps keep the muscles limber and tuned up compared to the same stiffening-up walk pace hour after hour.

The executive officer moves at the rear of the unit to account for and help with those troops falling back, and he keeps the commander up front informed as to how well the unit is doing in the rear. Ernie and I would usually meet toward the unit center during our rest breaks as he was on his feet checking on our Marines. I had no idea that the earlier humps were so hard on him until I walked into his office after a hike and found him flat on the deck with his bare feet up on a chair. His feet were covered with big red blisters, and I really felt for him. "Oh!" he said in answer to my concerned question, "I'm just a little slow in getting into Marine infantry shape. I'm okay. I'll be ready for next week's hump."

Ernie's headquarters staff job had allowed his feet to soften, and he told me that his desk work really didn't give him any worthwhile physical fitness time. All were reasons that he had sought a position within an infantry battalion. It took him awhile to get back in shape, but there was no slack in his duty performance while doing so. He would not have missed one of those painful hikes short of me ordering him to remain in the office, which I seriously considered. But at this stage in our relationship, I knew that he would resent and fight any such order. He was a doer.

Our battalion trained and got ready for our six-month deployment to Okinawa by undergoing and doing well on all of our predeployment evaluations and inspections. I had a great chance to use Major Van Huss' leadership abilities during our combined arms exercise (CAX) at our Marine Corps Base, Twenty-nine Palms, California. This was combined arms training and evaluation utilizing artillery and air support together on a target. My Marines did well through it all, as I describe in my memoir.

During our last day in the assault operation for which we were being evaluated, I elected to declare myself a casualty while I was away from the battalion on a chopper flight. Ernie got the word from headquarters that the enemy had knocked the chopper out of the sky and his commander was missing; he was now the battalion commander. He continued our action without a flaw. (This was all a surprise to him because I didn't give him any clue of my plan.) It was right down Ernie's alley. I knew he would love the opportunity. More than that, he surely deserved the chance to lead from the front.

Two months later our advance party with Ernie in charge left for Okinawa thirty days ahead of our battalion's movement. As a result of having his boots on the ground, we were provided with the information that the commanding general disliked facial hair on Marines. Ernie had our new home at Camp Schwab set up and all ready for us when we got there. My XO (as executive officers are called) was full of good ideas, and he wasn't bashful about presenting them. Fortunately for me I had an ear for his suggestions, and I provide two of them in the following paragraphs.

Ernie's first recommendation, upon learning that we would be assigned to the Fuji Base Camp for about ten days, was climbing Mount Fuji with our battalion. I loved the idea, but it had never approached my thoughts, and we probably never would have done it without Ernie's suggestion. In spite of his earlier foot problems, Ernie wanted to make the climb and knew that it would rate very high with me. We did it, and I relate the difficulties encountered during our climb up—including freezing temperatures and high wind on top, which caused three hypothermia cases during the short time we were up there—in my memoir.

Ernie's hang-in personality was with us all the way. He walked up through the ranks and checked on our Marines during my frequent halts for a quick rest in the course of the difficult climb. (We went up the back side of the mountain through deep, soft, sliding ash-sand.) My XO never sat down; he was always on the move, always checking on our Marines. He also later ensured that every Marine who made it to the top had an entry in his service record book crediting him with the climb.

The other outstanding suggestion Ernie made was that our battalion have an Asian-style Officers Mess Night there in Japan. His thoughts included wearing our field uniforms, using chopsticks, and being seated on the deck in one of the local restaurants. We did that and enjoyed great food, a relaxed evening, and the camaraderie of our fellow Marines. The high point of the evening was Ernie stripping to his bare chest, getting on the little stage, and challenging anyone to a wrestling match, sumo-style. Lieutenant Robert G. Burge quickly accepted the challenge, stripped to his waist, and entered the stage. Though Robert was in outstanding physical condition and a foot-plus taller than Ernie, he had less experience with this type of physical encounter. Ernie held his own and after a few minutes of roughing each other up, the two settled for a draw. They brought the house down with applause. Not only was it an entertaining show, but the act was completely unexpected. That night my officers really got to know each other, to appreciate our different personalities, and it was a grand opportunity for them to better know their second in command.

Major Van Huss' last surprise dropped on me was during my turnover of the battalion command to my replacement. Ernie was the commanding officer of troops, and at the proper time in the turnover ceremony he gave his command, "Deliver the colors to the commanding officer." Instantly the entire battalion shouted, "Attack! Attack! Attack!" Initially I was shocked with the outburst, but that shock quickly gave way to deep emotions. For a few seconds there, I wondered how I was going to be able to wipe my eyes in front of all the people in the reviewing stands. I didn't; I stood there watching the ceremony through tear-filled eyes. The word "attack" shouted three times had really become an emotional go-getter for my Marines over the year, and Ernie had it set to go for my departure. What a beautiful and emotional send off. Thank you, Ernie.

Personalities are what leadership is all about, and all people have a personality. Some wanna-be leaders might need to stop and take a look at who they really are, how others see them, and what changes they might want to work toward. If it is a personality that favors other people during the everyday events in life, then it is good to go. If it is all about "me," then that personality isn't going very far.

A very negative trait of a few people in positions over others is that awful word "deceitful." My second XO, the second in command, during my command of the Marine Corps Officer Candidates School at Quantico, had this problem. I was slow in accepting this fact about him, and in the process I handled it very poorly from the perspective of my junior officers.

Lieutenant Colonel Norman Wiggans held the position of XO when I assumed command, performed his duties in an outstanding manner, and completed his tour after my first year on the job. His replacement was accepted based upon a phone call from him to me. He was completing an overseas assignment and had orders for Quantico; he wanted to be XO of OCS. I considered one lieutenant colonel as good as the next, so I gave him the job. He was to report in about the same time Norm departed. We got along well enough. I had made it clear during our initial phone conversation that because our offices were small and adjoined that if he was a smoker, he wouldn't be able to smoke in his office. Yes, he smoked, he told me, but that would not be a problem. Our problem, of which I was at first unaware, must have been that he resented my method of leadership—or maybe me, for whatever reason. The situation never came to the point where I felt the need for a one-on-one with him; he did his job well enough. The deceitfulness took place behind my back.

As an example, during one of my officer meetings, he and I were seated side by side in front of our officers, who were facing us. At a point in my talk I was surprised to note bothered and concerned looks on several of my officers' faces, especially Major Mike Winter, my operations officer. (Winter was the lance corporal sniper involved in my fight on 22 February 1969 in Vietnam; he took over one of my radios and was seriously wounded by machine-gun fire a few minutes later.) They were all looking to my left, at the XO. Naturally, I looked to my left and wondered what they had seen. I let it ride because at the time I wasn't concerned.

Some time later Winter came into my office and asked for a private talk with me. I closed the door between the XO's office and mine. Mike related a negative statement the XO had made to our officers in reference to me. My approach has always been to lay it out before the involved parties, talk about it, clear it up. If there is a problem between individuals and they don't clear it up, there is no team. I opened the door and asked the XO to come in. He did so, and I informed him of what Mike had just told me. Naturally his position was that Mike and the other officers had misunderstood his words, and he cleared it up by telling me what he had intended to say.

Mike's information didn't concern me at the time because of the XO's explanation. But I did wrong by Mike; I should never have involved him directly with the XO. Thinking about that situation now, what I should have done was have a closed-door, sit-down talk with this XO and learn what his problem was. Later, I noticed that the XO went out of his way to befriend Mike. They often met in the smoking room for a cigarette and a bull session. I also was aware of a reduction in Mike's time with me. I blew that one.

After I became aware of the deceitful side of this XO, I realized that there was nothing I could do to influence or remake his personality. I simply ensured that his current rank was as high as he was going in our Marine Corps. The Corps didn't need him.

On the personality element of leadership, General Perry Smith addresses "Looking at Yourself" in his book *Rules and Tools for Leaders:* "Picture yourself surrounded by mirrors of many kinds. Some of the mirrors provide accurate reflections so that you can judge correctly your work as a leader. But a good number of the mirrors distort your image. Even the most consistent of leaders is understood in many different ways by many different people. Try to correct the worst of these distortions, whenever possible. . . . You are really five people: you are who you are; who you think you are; who your subordinates think you are; who your peers think you are; and who your superiors think you are. In many cases, there is a close relationship between and among the five 'you's.' Yet in other cases, the relationship is not close at all. Just as your qualities will be over-estimated or exaggerated in certain instances—you are probably not as good-looking, sexy, brilliant, witty, or charismatic as you sometimes think you are—there are times when you will be perceived, by yourself or by others, in a much less favorable light than deserved."

The general also provides his thoughts on integrity: "Leaders should not only talk about integrity but should operate at a high level of integrity. Furthermore, they should emphasize both personal and institutional integrity. Effective leaders take prompt corrective action when there are violations of integrity and upgrade the standards of institutional integrity over time. They also ensure that everybody understands his or her fundamental commitment to the values of the organization. Soon after assuming their leadership positions, leaders should look for ways to demonstrate such commitment. Institutional integrity cannot lie dormant until a crisis occurs; it must be ingrained and supported by leaders at all levels. Of all the qualities that a leader must have, integrity is the most important." I strongly recommend the "Integrity Check List" General Smith supplies in his book.

Colonel Don Myers, in his book *Leadership Defined,* also covers my point on personalities well, from both an institutional and individual perspective. Myers relates the following story as an illustration. He was checking out after finishing the Army's Advance Infantry and Jump Schools at Fort Benning, Georgia, and went to the Officers' Club to pay his bill:

> I told the woman behind the counter who I was, and that I was leaving the next day. Would she check my membership so that I could pay any bills that were due before I departed?
>
> She asked me if I had a note signed by a colonel. I asked why that was necessary, and she said that it would verify that I was actually leaving. I took a deep breath, and then very calmly and deliberately explained that I was a captain in the Marines, and that I did not need a note from anyone to verify that I was telling the truth. She could tell me what my bill was and I would pay it, or she could have it forwarded to my next duty station, and I would return a check. I had no intention of having anyone verify my integrity.
>
> At this time another woman approached the counter and told the first woman that it was not necessary for Marines to have a colonel sign a note. That was only for Army officers. Perhaps in the past there had been a problem with a few officers trying to avoid paying monthly dues, but that is no excuse to question the integrity of all.

Don is right on with the way it used to be, and I hope it is still that way in the Marine Corps. Back in my time a Marine officer in uniform never produced an identification card for cashing personal checks, paying bills, checking out weapons and equipment, or any other reason at one of our Marine Corps bases. Maybe now that any person can buy any uniform desired from many sources, things have changed and identifying oneself is necessary. However, for the sake of the Marine Corps and Marines, I hope that there has not been a change.

Knowledge

8

> I can't say enough about the two Marine Divisions.
> If I use words like "brilliant" it would really be an
> under description of the absolutely superb job that
> they did in breaching the so-called impenetrable
> barrier. It was a classic—absolutely classic—military
> breaching of a very tough mine field, barb-wire, fire
> trenches–type barrier.
>
> *General Norman Schwarzkopf*

eing prepared tactically and technically to do the job, having the ability and knowledge to take on the task and to accomplish the mission, is a requirement of those in positions of leadership. Positive leadership—from the bottom leader to the one at the top—demands this ability. Though I was aware of the impressive leadership provided by my squad leader in the Korean War, we, the gunfighters, were lacking in some major areas needed to conduct successful infantry warfare. This was due for the most part to higher-level leadership shortfalls. Yes, we did the job anyway, but at what price?

No doubt many of our leaders knew what had to be done, how to train us, and what our equipment needs were. But in this case knowledge of our needs was not the problem. There were reasons for our shortfalls in the Korean War, the primary one being the lack of information, which might have been supplied by past leaders. The Marine Corps following World War II had been reduced from just under 600,000 Marines to fewer than 68,000 by 1950. President Harry S. Truman had decided that there was no longer a need for infantry fighters. The next war, if any, would be a push-button war, and the new U.S. Air Force would handle it. Our Congress obviously was somewhat supportive of this decision, though it didn't completely do away with the Marine Corps, even though that was President Truman's wish.

Shortly after June 1950, General Douglas MacArthur found the new Korean War going very badly for him and his army of occupational forces on the ground because they couldn't stop the North Korean aggressor. He had to have Marines, warriors who knew how to fight, could fight, and would fight. A Marine division with an air wing and supporting forces was therefore assigned to the Korean theater. The Marines turned the war around for MacArthur, but that situation placed the rest of the Marine Corps on hard rock for a period of time. I won't get into related stateside issues, such as my senior drill instructor's rank was corporal, E-3, and our junior drill instructor had graduated from boot camp only several months before me. Also, there were activated Marine Reservists who had never attended Marine Corps boot camp but found themselves on the ground and involved in the Korean War.

Recruits during my enlistment time went to the Korean War with only boot camp training; the Marine Corps did not have a separate unit and the time to provide new Marines with infantry training. We got one week of infantry training at Parris Island's Elliott Beach during our boot camp time of eleven weeks, and that was it. And in Platoon 88's case, that amounted to nothing, as I relate in my memoir. Yes, we did chase and catch a few rabbits for our senior drill instructor, but Corporal Reiser obviously knew nothing about infantry tactics.

When I arrived in Korea in January 1951, the 1st Marine Division had been through the fighting in the Pusan Perimeter, the Inchon amphibious landing, the battle for Seoul, and the fight out of the Chosin Reservoir. Casualties had reduced the force and replacements were badly needed, now. So I and many other new Marines went to Korea on what could be considered "the overnight express." As if that was not bad enough, Marine leadership at all levels suffered, not only in numbers but also in experience.

The Marine Corps was playing catch-up through all ranks and command positions. Due to the earlier downsizing of the Corps and the short time span of the new need, only a few leaders were school trained. Lieutenants were commissioned from the enlisted ranks, and many of the officers and staff noncommissioned officers during my time were activated Marine Reservists. Most of the lieutenants commissioned from the enlisted ranks (such as my platoon commander, Lieutenant Brimmer) knew and understood leadership and did a commendable job as commanders of rifle platoons and companies in that war.

Reserve officers (especially those who had been involved in World War II) performed well, but their interest and focus several months earlier had been in other areas, their family and their business or job. Now they were committed and involved in something that was not on their druthers list. They probably had stayed in the Reserves because their new family needed the extra money and they figured there would be no more wars. And like me and other recruits who were short on infantry training, some leaders were unprepared for their assignment in combat positions and had no adjustment time. Though I wasn't knowledgeable enough to know it at the time, shortfalls due to the lack of better higher-level leadership, meaning leaders with the knowledge of how to prepare us for what was facing us, included the following.

TEST FIRING AND ZEROING OF WEAPONS

We were issued M-1 Garand rifles at Camp Lejeune and took them to Korea with us. The M-1 is a gas-operated, clip-fed, air-cooled, semiautomatic shoulder weapon and a good rifle. We went to the range at Camp Lejeune and zeroed-in our rifles, which amounted to learning where our rifle sights had to be set in order to hit targets at different ranges of fire, say, distances of one hundred and two hundred yards. Shooting at targets naturally included the knowledge that the rifle worked as expected, known as test firing. But our experience with the Garands ended there.

In Korea we fired our weapons only when we had the enemy in our sights. Upon joining my rifle squad, I requested and was given the Browning automatic rifleman position, giving up my M-1. I only fired at the enemy using the rifle for that position, the Browning automatic, caliber .30, M1918A2, an air-cooled, gas-operated, magazine-fed shoulder weapon with bipod. There was no test firing and no learning the zero of the rifle or sight setting. Of course, with this rifle, every fifth round was a tracer bullet so I always knew what and where my bullets were hitting. I could easily adjust my fire on a target in the same manner as with a machine gun (or, for example, as with a garden hose with water). You see where you are hitting, raise, lower, or move right or left as needed to hit your target.

However, the lack of test firing and learning the zero of my rifle really hit home several months later when I was moved to a fire-team leader position and had to give up my Browning automatic and carry an M-1 again. I relate these experiences in my memoir; suffice it to say here, a squad of Chinese soldiers escaped from my full clip of ammo (eight rounds) fired at them from their flank at about two hundred yards. They continued to live because I did not know the zero or sight setting of the M-1 for the range (distance) from me to them. They were close enough as they walked unconcerned on my flank and presented good, slow-moving targets so that I should have hit more than the one I did. The thought of raising my sights to account for the distance never occurred to me; I did not know what that setting was. This action was the first time I had fired that rifle.

At another time a Chinese soldier lived a few minutes longer because my M-1 rifle misfired when I squeezed the trigger with him in my rifle sights as he charged toward us. (I had replaced the earlier M-1 with a casualty's rifle, but there was still no opportunity for test firing and sight setting.) My buddy, Estel Tuggle, in a shallow hole on my right, was seriously wounded by a grenade thrown by this Chinese soldier two seconds later. Correcting my rifle's failure to feed problem, I dropped that soldier as he ran from us, but that was no help for Tuggle. If I had only known that my rifle wasn't feeding ammo into the chamber correctly! Test firing our rifles would not have cost us anything in time or energy, and Tuggle would not have lost his leg.

Rifle ranges, of course, were not available to us in Korea, but we could have covered that shortfall easily enough. Periodically, we would be pulled off the front line for rest and nourishment in a mission known as "reserve"—a battalion, regiment, and even once our division was placed in Corps reserve. In Korea these reserve positions were behind the front line (friendly side) with no enemy threat to us. If nothing else, we could have placed empty C-ration boxes out in the rice paddies or on a hillside and fired at them. The distance away, one and two hundred yards, would give us the rifle's zero for hitting a target at that particular range as well as the knowledge that the weapon worked as expected. Why didn't we do that?

In my next war, Vietnam, my Alpha Company Marines did it. We took advantage of every opportunity to work with our weapons. Many times that included firing at boxes out in the rice paddies. We always knew our weapons, their sight settings, and their capability.

LACK OF INFANTRY TACTICS

My rifle platoon in the Korean War took all of our assigned objectives. The heavy or difficult objectives were handled in the same formation and manner that we used to secure the easier ones. Our assault formation was always a column of files, meaning a one-man front. Why? We didn't know any better. We obviously were short in leader knowledge as well as individual knowledge. Half of the Marines of my squad were recruits like me with no infantry training, and the remainder were activated weekend warriors, Reservists with not much more training.

Corporal Davis was one of three in the squad who were Marines before the war broke out and were properly trained. However, and I never really thought about it until this writing, Davis' military occupational specialty was refrigeration repair man, not infantry. Though he was a great leader, he, to my knowledge, never exercised tactical formation control of us. He never corrected or suggested any change to our single-file assault up those ridges, although he was always right in there and involved with us.

Another factor that influenced the shape of our formation was the terrain. The narrow ridgelines we assaulted did not lend themselves to much of an on-line assault formation. One behind the other, a one-man front, was the easiest way to control the squad. In my next war we assaulted many ridgelines, and some in the A Shau Valley were as narrow as the Korean ridges. However, I always had at least a fire team on line, a four-man front, if not a squad of thirteen on those ridges.

CHECKING POSITIONS AT NIGHT

Leader knowledge includes knowing what is taking place within the organization one leads at all times—the good and bad situations, during the easy times as well as the tough ones. Throughout my nine months in an infantry squad on the front line in the Korean War, I never knew of any leader checking our positions on the line, the MLR, ensuring that the watch standers were awake and alert. If the watch stander dozed off, his only concern was the enemy. Sometimes my fighting hole would be located in a most unlikely avenue of approach for the enemy due to extremely rough terrain and ground cover, and because of the unlikely threat the enemy thus posed, if my foxhole buddy failed to awaken me for my watch (which happened a number of times), I slept. Of course I would soon wake anyway, check my watch for the time, and realize my buddy had failed to wake me.

My screwed-up reasoning at the time was that it was my buddy's fault should the platoon leader or platoon sergeant by chance check on us. The watch responsibility had not been passed to me, and my buddy should suffer the consequences of sleeping on watch, not me. I always stood my watches, but when I passed the watch to him, I was relieved of the duty until he passed it back to me. Again, because of our location, with the rough terrain around us and the black of the night, I was not concerned with the enemy finding us even if they did assault our hill. Our leader also would have had a difficult time moving from hole to hole; maybe that was the reason we never saw him, or our squad leader, after sleep time. But that was negative knowledge, not knowledge we could positively live by.

The knowledge that no leader had ever approached us in the dark of night was a negative factor with regard to our individual security and unit defense.

Machine-gun crews had at least four Marines with which to share the one-man watch on the gun throughout the night, compared to two riflemen in a fighting hole with one on watch at a time. I suspect that many nights the gun watch standers (two guns per platoon) were the only ones awake on our platoon front, especially after a long, hard day of moving forward in the assault mode.

In chapter 10 and in my memoir I relate different stories about my rifle company in the Vietnam War, including a story about catching a machine-gun watch stander asleep in his bunker. Leaders have to be knowledgeable and proficient all the way around, day and night and in all areas. That knowledge, or the lack thereof, is easily read by all followers. My basic point with being tactically and technically proficient is that leaders must know their job, know their people, and be physically involved with them; this helps the followers to know what is expected of them and what to expect from their leaders.

Good leaders know that all members of the team have something to add and contribute to the mission's accomplishment. However, the leader has to have an ear for these contributions, and the followers need to know that their leader is open to and will consider their suggestions. I'll make my point with an event that happened in my rifle company on Operation Dewey Canyon during the Vietnam War.

Two mornings after our big fight on 22 February 1969 in the A Shau Valley, my Alpha Company was dug in with defensive positions on a ridgeline. We were recuperating from our loss two days before, from wounds not serious enough to warrant evacuation, from the loss of our Marine buddies (twelve killed [including two officers] and fifty-four [two more officers] evacuated for fear of loss of life or limb), and from working with and getting to know the Marine replacements who had just joined us. The enlisted Marines were fresh over from the States, but the lieutenants had been with Alpha Company during their first six months in country and had been assigned rear-area jobs for their last six months. They heard of my loss and volunteered to return to Alpha Company and the bush, and I was pleased to receive them.

The North Vietnamese Army held reveille on Alpha Company that second morning on that ridge. They had moved to a ridgeline about three hundred meters away and at the same height as our position on our ridge. At the first light of dawn, they opened up on Alpha's position with automatic weapons and rifle-propelled grenades (RPGs). They held their fire on us for about a minute and then cut it off. By the time I got return fire on their position, they were gone. My Alpha Marines were all sleeping below ground level, and those on watch were in their fighting holes, so we were not hurt. The following morning, the enemy did the very same thing. Again there was no loss on our side other than loss of sleep with the early reveille. That evening one of my replacement lieutenants approached me with a recommendation: "Sir, why don't we zero all weapons on the position the enemy fire has come from and just before daylight open up with everything we have?"

"No, Lieutenant," I replied, "they are never in the same place twice once we learn where they are located."

My initial thought was that the lieutenant's suggestion was no use because the enemy knew we would be ready for him. Then it hit me: Hell, the enemy just did it again this morning, two days in a row. I changed my mind: "Good thought, Lieutenant! We'll do that if for no other reason than we have nothing better to do." I registered my mortars and machine guns on that ridge before dark and directed all riflemen on that side of our defense to take that ridge under fire when our mortar tubes popped the next morning. We were not bothered with any enemy action during the night, so all weapons remained trained and zeroed in on that ridge.

The next morning, just as I expected the first light to break on our ridge, I gave the command "Fire" over my radio to the mortar section and my machine guns. As directed all of my riflemen opened fire along with the mortars and machine guns. What a noise! I cut it off with a command to "cease fire" after one minute. We heard and saw nothing from that ridge other than some small brush fires.

I assumed that the enemy had not moved up for a repeat, but after about an hour, I sent a rifle squad on patrol in that direction to check it out. They found a mess of human bodies; the North Vietnamese Army unit had planned and was in position to do it a third time. Their weapons were in position for firing but there was no one alive. I couldn't believe they would try the same thing three times straight. Thanks, Lieutenant, you had a great idea.

Hans Finzel, in his book *The Top Ten Mistakes Leaders Make*, is right on the subject:

> Here's the profile of an ideal supervisor developed by a group of supervisors participating in a training workshop on discipline at Brookdale Hospital Medical Center. Supervisors were asked to identify what they felt were ten

major functions of an effective supervisor and to rank the functions in order of importance. Effective supervisors:

Delegate authority in areas affecting their work;

Consult with subordinates before making decisions pertaining to their job responsibilities;

Give employees the reason for implementing decisions;

Don't play favorites;

Praise excellent work;

Reprimand subordinates who fail to observe the proper chain-of-command relationships;

Never reprimand or discipline in front of coworkers;

Encourage employees to offer their opinions and criticisms of supervisory policies;

Listen to employees' explanations before placing blame in disciplinary situations; accept reasonable explanations, not excuses; obey all the rules that subordinates are expected to obey.

I again strongly urge young leaders to study General Perry Smith's "Leadership Skills Checklist" in his book *Rules and Tools for Leaders.* He writes: "The enhancement of leadership skills will improve your effectiveness, your time management, and your quality of life."

Knowledge is an essential element of leadership, and it covers a broad plain. A good leader knows how to prepare for the assigned or assumed task, what is needed to support his or her effort, and how to move forward in accomplishing the mission. Equally important to the leader is understanding and knowing his or her followers, their individual strengths and weaknesses. All good leaders should know what to do in any situation and be keenly aware of his or her personal strengths and weaknesses.

Motivation

9

You do not lead by hitting people over the head—
that is assault, not leadership.

General Dwight D. Eisenhower

If you want to be a leader and you work a little harder than the average team member toward your unit's mission or purpose, you can reach your goal. Another requirement for attaining a leadership position is the recognition of the contributions and capabilities of the other team members. When your colleagues and co-workers look to you for guidance with the next step in their endeavors, you have arrived on leadership's doorstep. An individual's level of motivation toward accomplishing any challenge is key to how that challenge will end, and motivation is easily recognized by those with whom you are involved. When we want something strongly enough, we usually get it, and that is what leading others is all about: "The difficult we do immediately; the impossible takes a little longer."

I experienced an excellent example of the subject of this chapter in the Vietnam War. My Alpha Company was set up on Hill 37 just west of the Cam Lo village in the I Corps tactical zone with the mission of area security. This amounted to conducting reconnaissance/combat patrols and employing nightly ambushes within our tactical area of operation (TAOR). Operation Dewey Canyon in the A Shau Valley was behind us; we had rested up and filled our depleted ranks with replacement infantry Marines from the States. Our problem at this time was that we were not having any enemy contact, in spite of our lengthy, daily patrols and night ambush operations.

There were enemy forces in the area, though they were low in numbers. They obviously knew our routine because we were doing pretty much what other rifle companies had done with this assignment over the years before us. The enemy knew when and how we patrolled and the routes we traveled that returned us to Hill 37 before dark. We had our favorite ambush positions at night; all major intersections of road and trails were targets. In spite of our active operations, we learned that North Vietnamese Army personnel visited different parts of the Cam Lo village at night for food and whatever. Because of years of repetition and routine, they knew when and what to expect from us and were able to carry on with their visits to other little villages in our TAOR as well as Cam Lo.

I decided that we needed another way of performing our mission, one that I hoped had never been used here. After some serious thoughts on the subject, my solution to our problem was the employment of hunter-killer teams within our TAOR. Alpha Company's TAOR covered about four square miles of land, including the Cam Lo River. That was a big area for a rifle company of less than two hundred Marines to cover every hour of the day and night. Instead of day patrols and night ambushes, my hunter-killer teams took over, not just for the day or the night, but for two days and two nights.

I broke my tactical area down into squad areas with boundaries that were identified by landmarks such as trails, roads, creeks, unique rice paddies, and anything else identifiable. I ensured that a buffer zone lay between the squad areas in operation because friendly fire is as deadly as the enemy's fire. With a no-man's land between the operational squad areas, I thought it would work safely enough. I didn't sleep very soundly the first couple of nights my squads were out, but the plan worked well and safely for my Marines. The squad-assigned areas were changed weekly and no-man's land was never the same two weeks straight. The enemy had a tough time figuring out a safe passage because we constantly changed our patrol and ambush areas.

My young squad leaders, many of them lance corporals, jumped at the opportunity of being totally responsible for their operation. (I suppose their experience was similar to my squad leader responsibility on that distant out-post mission in the Korean War: There was no one looking over their shoulder telling them what to do and how to do it.) They were motivated and readily accepted the operational idea, the responsibility, and the operation. My young leaders moved their squads into their area of operation one night, set up ambushes as desired, moved to another position offering better opportunities as desired, and before daylight moved into their hideaway for the day. Their day position was chosen based on which location offered the best opportunity to observe all activity taking place within their area of operation during the day, which would allow them to choose their following night ambush sites.

The assigned area belonged to the squad leader; anyone they saw was enemy, so it was shoot first, search the bodies later. (There was a curfew in effect that prevented civilians from outside movement or activity during darkness.) Artillery and Marine air could not fire into their area without the squad leader's approval, and that was coordinated through my company artillery and air forward observers. It worked and it worked well. Our enemy body count jumped up by 200 percent, and at no cost to my Marines. This was new to the enemy. They couldn't figure out what was going on, what trails were safe, and when the Marine would be back on Hill 37.

Young, motivated leaders will take it to the top when given the opportunity and trust, especially when it is a break from a routine that has gotten old and nonproductive. Young men and especially Marines love to engage in new and worthwhile endeavors. My squad leaders and squad members were equally motivated with our hunter-killer team operations. They didn't get much sleep and had fewer rations and water (other than local water in the creeks and streams, which had to be treated), but they were inspired and looked forward to their days and nights out. Their squad efforts were productive, they were getting a return for their efforts, and the cost was only a little "do without" on their personal comfort side. We suffered no casualties during this time.

I recently read the 2006 book *Tiger Force* by Michael Sallah and Mitch Weiss, the true story of an Army regiment's experimental fighting unit in the Vietnam War, May to November 1967. Tiger Force was one reconnaissance platoon (about forty-five soldiers) within the 1st Battalion of the 327th Infantry Regiment. I understand that other Army units conducted operations using Tiger Force's method of free action within a free-fire zone (which basically was "do whatever you want"). Motivation of a kind was involved here, including at the battalion and regiment levels. While I consider motivation an essential element of leadership, motivation also needs positive, on-hand guidance. The Tiger Force personnel make my point well.

Tiger Force was given a long leash and allowed to operate in the field with no supervision. Yes, they had a platoon commander—Lieutenant James Hawkins, who not only ordered his men to kill the innocent but also led in the number of innocents killed—but the problem was the lack of leadership up the chain of command, including the battalion commander and higher. No commander, other than the one assigned to the platoon, was ever in the field with Tiger Force. The higher commanders controlled the action by radio, and that usually amounted to demanding a body count. The area had been determined a free-fire zone, and some of the Tiger Force personnel took that as a license to kill babies, women, old people, and anything that moved.

"What happened during the seven months Tiger Force descended into the abyss is the stuff of nightmares," the authors relate. "Their crimes were unaccountable, their madness beyond imagination—so much so that for almost four decades, the story of Tiger Force was covered up under orders that stretched all the way to the White House. Records were scrubbed, documents were destroyed, and men were told to say nothing."

We all have heard of the My Lai massacre in the Vietnam War and Lieutenant William Calley's negative leadership at the rifle platoon level and his company commander's lack of involvement and knowledge as to what was taking place with his troops. There were many other people in leadership positions involved in the Calley incident who didn't know what was going on within their force. Twenty-eight officers, including two generals, were involved in the cover-up of the massacre, but none, other than Calley, were ever convicted. The My Lai massacre, however, took place on one operation on one day, not on numerous operations over a period of seven months. Tiger Force is another example of a major lack of forward, on-hand, positive leadership exercised by those who are responsible. There was no one on hand to say no.

I suppose motivation is involved here, but certainly the wrong kind. Some of those men in uniform were not mentally qualified to wear the uniform in the first place. (Some of them were no doubt enlistees in Secretary of Defense Robert McNamara's Project One Hundred Thousand.) The problem was compounded when there were no real leaders to focus, guide, and direct their personal motivation. This wasn't so much of a team action as it was individuals doing what was the easiest for them, doing as they desired. It was much easier to squeeze a trigger than try to get a helicopter in to evacuate the people while having to provide security for all of that. An evacuation effort would cut into personal time, chow, rest, and sleep.

The authors of *Tiger Force* identify a number of these soldiers, many of whom suffered the post-traumatic stress disorder and several who died later at home under the age of fifty. No wonder. Those who didn't go along with and participate in the killings had to live with what the few killers within the team did. Those who pulled the triggers had a heavier load on their brain, and it would show, even while they still served with Tiger Force. It got to the point that killing became automatic. See a person? Shoot him or her, regardless. The worst individual, Sam Ybarra, who should never have been allowed to wear a uniform, was really a mental case; he took his crimes to the grave with him, at home while still in his thirties.

Obviously not all PTSD patients were murderers. Some suffer because of their mental makeup and outlook on life; they can't accept or put to rest what they have seen and experienced. Not everyone possesses the mental makeup to be a good soldier, and some suffer the consequences of having to do the soldier's job. Then there are those who later feel guilt for not doing their share in the team's fight against the enemy for whatever reason, maybe concern for self or not seeing an easy, positive way to help. Others may be faced with the realization that their noninvolvement in the firefight could have cost others their lives, and as a result they suffer from PTSD.

I also wonder how many of these PTSD cases receiving full benefits from the Veterans Administration were never in or near a firefight but served in some support activity far in the rear with the gear, in safety. The Veterans Administration even pays PTSD medical allowance to some who never served with any military or naval service, never wore a uniform (see B. G. Burkett and Glenna Whitley's 1998 book *Stolen Valor: How the Vietnam Generation Was Robbed of Its Heroes and Its History*).

A good soldier with the proper childhood experiences, good military training, love of country, and acceptance of the mission as a team member is not likely to suffer post-traumatic stress disorder. He does what is expected of him, what he was trained to do, and the bottom line is that it's either him or the enemy soldier. War has been among us for a long time now. There are no warriors that desire war; their purpose is to end it, if not to keep it from starting in the first place.

Those Vietnamese country people who suffered from the actions of Tiger Force knew no other life. They had spent their entire existence in their little hamlets with their rice paddies, and they were not about to leave their homes for the unknown. The armed forces moved many out of harm's way, but some didn't stay removed; they returned to their homes. The U.S. and South Vietnamese armed forces were no different than the Viet Cong and North Vietnamese forces to these country people. Both forces were against them and interfered with their way of life.

Our Marines had a different approach to the Vietnamese country people within the Marine area of responsibility. In what was known as the Combined Action Program (CAP), they placed Marine squad-sized units within the Vietnamese villages. The Marines became the police force, if not part of the people of the village. Marines didn't kill the people; they worked with and provided for them. My feelings are that if we had used this CAP approach throughout Vietnam, the war would have had a very different ending.

I suppose it is a good thing I was not aware in 1969 of Tiger Force's operations, because if I had been, I may never have gone with my hunter-killer team idea. My Marines, however, would never have considered such a thing as killing the innocent. If one individual had gone off the deep end, become a killer, his buddies would have had him corrected posthaste. My motivated lance corporal squad leaders would never have condoned such action. I for sure would have known about such a thing if it ever had happened, within minutes of the action, and I didn't look over my junior leaders' shoulders. The Marine Corps' screening of recruits in boot camp also ensures that we don't have this mentality within our ranks; individual and leader motivation, yes, we have it, and the right kind.

As in all past wars, Marine rifle company commanders in the Vietnam War followed in trace of their lead or assault platoon with the rest of their company moving behind them. Rifle platoon leaders did the same; they were always behind their lead or assault squad. This assures that the leader knows what is going on and, with two-thirds of his force behind him, can determine how he is going to influence the outcome of the mission.

Some motivated combat leaders have moved forward and become directly involved in the action, the firefights. What is best for the unit, the team, and the individual Marines? Is it the leader's direct involvement in the firefight as another rifleman or is it in the position of providing guidance and direction for the team, the force? Leaving the team without a leader is not good, and that easily can happen if the leader gets too involved in the riflemen's business. A leader must not get into a situation where he cannot move and communicate with his force, such as being pinned down under heavy enemy small-arms and machine-gun fire. The issue really boils down to what is best for the leader's unit—a display of the warrior's courage at that moment or having a leader tomorrow and throughout the fight.

History has plenty of examples of inspirational leaders who moved forward and got their force out of the trenches. Sergeant Major Dan Daly, USMC, in the Belleau Woods battle of World War I, did that when he left his trench shouting, "Come on you sons of bitches, do you want to live forever?" Second Lieutenant Henry A. Commiskey, USMC, in his rifle platoon's assault on an enemy position near Yongdungp'o in the Korean War, was the first fighter to enter the enemy defense. He received the Medal of Honor for killing many enemy soldiers in that fight. What was his platoon of riflemen doing at the time? Wouldn't it have hurt the enemy more if each of his riflemen had fought as he did? It is only in last-ditch situations, where there is not much hope of a tomorrow, that a motivated leader is justified in stepping in front of his force with a "Follow me!" My battalion lost two officers, a captain who was a rifle company commander and a major who was the battalion operations officer, on Operation Dewey Canyon because they stepped forward. Their stories are covered in chapter 13.

On several occasions in the Vietnam War, my company was on a patrol or in movement to contact when my lead platoon took a wrong turn or trail. Following my lead platoon, my country boy background and Korean War experience would cause me to recognize the correct trail, almost totally covered by foliage, as I approached it in our direction of movement. I would lead my company on the correct trail rather than continue to follow my lead platoon. After a few minutes I would realize that walking point, the first rifleman in the forward-moving formation, was not a good position for the company commander because the first enemy rounds would make this company leaderless until the XO could move forward from his position in the rear and take control. I would hold up my movement and wait for the original lead platoon (which had gotten back on this trail) to catch up.

The motivation within the individual for a particular event or situation helps make a leader. If you want something strongly enough, you go for it, and it is that involvement that tends to make you a leader. Two good examples of this involvement happened during my sport parachuting life. I had been parachuting, both military and sport, for several years before my nineteen-month tour of duty in the Vietnam War. The war was a long break in my parachuting experiences, and I looked forward to getting back in the air upon reporting in for duty at our Marine Corps base in Quantico. I knew there was a very good and active sport parachute club there. I had made a few guest jumps with them in the past.

After getting settled in with my new duties and my family home situation in 1970, I sought information on the jump club and attended the weekly club meeting. Much to my disappointment upon arriving at the clubhouse, the two club members in attendance informed me that they were the club. They were the only two members, and they jumped with the nearest civilian club at a small air field in Stafford County. The Marine Corps did not support the club, and the helicopter squadron on Quantico, HMX-1, would not provide choppers for club use.

The sergeant who was the club president stated that he was meeting tonight with the other member only to dissolve the club. There was no purpose or reason to continue with a club that had no aircraft support, which was the reason, in the first place, Marines were not interested in joining the club. I could not believe what I was hearing; surely someone had dropped the ball along the line. The Marine Corps' earlier commitment to the Vietnam War no doubt was a factor, but the war situation was lightening up for Marines, including Marine Air. At this time, I thought, maybe we could get aircraft support if someone pursued it. I wanted to give it a try, and I asked the sergeant if he would consider not dissolving the club. I told him I wanted to join it. He said, "Sure, Captain, if you want this mess here you can have it, and we two club members elect you as the club president. It is all yours and we wish you the best."

I visited the HMX-1 operations officer the next day with positive result. The major responded to my request with "Yes, Captain, I'll give you a Ch-46 with two gas loads every other Saturday. Will that work? Now, as to the pilots, Saturdays are their personal time, so you will have to get your pilots on a volunteer basis. I will not task the flight crew for your club jumping. Okay?"

The major also gave me a list of the HMX-1 pilots with a notation by those who might want or need the extra flight time. It worked. The first pilot I called was ready whenever I needed him. My next act was to get membership in the club; we had to have jumpers. The base newspaper, the *Quantico Sentinel*, was a big help with this. It gave our reactivated club several write ups that informed young Marines wanting to jump from an aircraft in flight how to join.

Lieutenants at the Basic School filled the club's ranks, and it was no time before I was heavily involved in conducting parachute jump training. The word got out, and experienced jumpers sought out and joined the new Quantico Sport Parachute Club; they also helped with the organization's business. Our club membership quickly increased to thirty-five members, most of them beginners. Along with running the parachute club, I continued with the training and jump-master duties for my entire tour of duty at Quantico. Motivation will carry one well down the leader's trail.

An assignment to duty in Europe followed my Quantico tour, and for those two years my parachuting was very limited. My next duty assignment was to the 3rd Marine Division on Okinawa, and I held high hopes of getting back in the air once I got there. This was another of those Marine Corps unaccompanied tours (one's family has to remain in the States); my evenings and weekends were entirely mine. Jumping helped fill the void of family life.

I was assigned to the 3rd Reconnaissance Battalion, which had a deep reconnaissance platoon as a result of the deactivation of the 1st Force Reconnaissance Company. The deep reconnaissance platoon needed a jump master, and I was the only one in the battalion, so I got some Marine Corps jumps. I also wanted to get involved with the division's Sport Parachute Club for weekend activities. Our battalion was located at Onna Point on the western coast of Okinawa, and I learned that the sport club was at Camp Hansen on the eastern coast. Unable to get any information on the club by phone, the next Saturday I crossed the mountain between our bases on my motorcycle to visit Camp Hansen and the club.

My second experience of becoming involved in a nonfunctioning organization happened on Okinawa. As at Quantico in 1970, the 3rd Marine Division's Sport Parachute Club had folded. There were no club members at the clubhouse, and worse, there were no club members because there was no Marine aircraft support. The clubhouse was full of parachutes and equipment. I located the base official who had the key to the clubhouse and went to work. There obviously had been a lack of leadership motivation somewhere along the way. Some leader did not go the distance to work out the use of Marine helicopters. Several squadrons were there on the island with us, and like us, the pilots and crew had not much more to do with their spare time. Pilots like to add up their flight time. They too were without their families.

As I had done earlier at Quantico, I visited the helicopter squadron operations officer and received chopper support on each weekend, Saturdays and sometimes on Sundays. In no time I had the club back in operation and membership—both trained parachutists and those wanting to be trained—rapidly increased. Two evenings each week were consumed with conducting parachute training, and my weekends were filled with jump-master duties during jump operations. Motivation takes one the distance.

Most of us at different times have, or at least feel that we have, a better way of doing the task at hand as laid out before us. That is great because the more thought and input on an issue by individuals, the better the end results. We are not all alike in our thought processes, not all schooled, trained, and prepared to do the same task in a like manner. And that is what makes a team, a society, and any organization work so well. Someone, if not several someones, will have a better, easier way of accomplishing a specific mission.

Once a decision is made by the senior leader, however, all minds at all levels of leadership must be on the same track. Hopefully he or she has considered all individual input and included the recommendations in the plan where they work best. He or she then issues the order: "Do It!" Subordinate leaders must take that superior's decision as their own and move forward with it. A subordinate leader may not be aware of all of the issues the senior has considered in making a decision. While a subordinate leader may have his own ideas regarding a particular issue, he should use these only as they fit within the scheme of the senior's directions. He must keep in mind that he is only one cog in that drive wheel moving forward. He probably does not know what some of the other cogs are facing in regard to endurance, capabilities, knowledge, strength, equipment or weapons, and opposition. The leader at the top should have a better handle on all of these subjects.

My Marine Corps method was this: Orders issued to me were my orders to my Marines, not a pass-down such as "the colonel wants us to. . . ." My fellow officers behaved the same, though we might, depending on the situation and the details of the order, have the option to add and modify to the mission as we moved forward. Situations change as we begin to accomplish a mission, and allowing subordinate commanders the freedom and opportunity to change as required is a sound principle. Combat, for example, is a fluid, constantly moving situation, and leaders at all levels must be able to react as the situation changes in order to take advantage of all intelligence on the enemy force as it becomes available. But this is not always the case. The bottom line is that the task and mission goals laid out by the senior authority remain as the team's goals for each subordinate commander.

An instance of a subordinate leader not following the commander's mission goals happened at a U.S. Marine Security Guard unit in one of our embassies during my tour of duty as the executive officer of Company A, Marine Security Guard Battalion. Company A's headquarters was located in Frankfurt, Germany, and my tour of duty was June 1972 to June 1974. My primary duty was inspecting the Marines at each of our embassies. We had a Marine detachment in a capital city of one of the major countries of Western Europe with a staff sergeant in charge. All detachments were run by a staff noncommissioned officer, and the more Marines assigned, the higher the senior's rank.

This particular staff sergeant had his own ideas of how he would run his detachment. Company, battalion, and Marine Corps orders and regulations covered all aspects of the Marine Security Guard business, from the requirement to maintain and run the Marine House where they all lived to personal conduct and performance of their guard duties in the embassy. But in spite of these specific directives, this staff noncommissioned officer in charge came up with his own way of running his detachment. After all, he was out there by himself, a long way from anyone senior to him.

The staff sergeant felt that his Marines were overworked. Their mission was security of the embassy, which in those days amounted to a guard on duty when the embassy was closed, basically nights and weekends. That was our routine in those days, and four Marine guards plus a staff sergeant were the number of Marines assigned to the smaller embassies. For the guards that amounted to security duty every other night and every other weekend, usually four hours on watch and four off.

To give his Marines even more time off, the staff sergeant knocked off general military subject training, which took place during the weekdays for those Marines not on that day's guard roster. He relaxed the personal accountability of his Marines, and he no longer inspected the Marine house for cleanliness and order. He looked the other way when a Marine got out of line by drinking too much alcohol or became involved with other personal problems.

The problem came to the attention of the embassy security officer, who called Frankfurt. We had a serious problem. I flew up for an investigation and quickly learned its cause. The staff sergeant was relieved of duty and returned to the States. Our problem went away.

As Hans Finzell states in his *Top Ten Mistakes Leaders Make*, "Rather than always dictating decisions, a good leader will try as often as possible to let those he is leading make decisions. Insisting on being in on all the decisions communicates lack of trust and confidence. It also slows the development of new leadership. Very often *how* a project is done doesn't really matter. If it is done differently but accomplished effectively, then the job gets done, which is all that matters."

And regarding this essential element of leadership, Major General Smith notes in his *Rules and Tools for Leaders*, "Leaders who truly share their power can accomplish extraordinary things. The best leaders understand that leadership is the liberation of talent; they gain power not only by constantly giving it away, but also by not grabbing it back. Making empowerment stick requires much candid discussion, trust, and interaction between leaders and subordinate associates."

Individual motivation is affected in many ways, both negatively and positively. I think I was a pretty good Marine in the Korean War, including when I performed my leadership duties. But I experienced a negative time there, caused by the loss of personal motivation. I returned to my Item Company following my wound recovery in June, but due to the unit's needs, I was assigned to the 2nd Platoon rather than my 3rd Platoon. I had looked forward to getting back with my squad, my family. I wanted to know who we lost in our assault on that machine gun and who was still in our squad.

I didn't know anyone in the 2nd Platoon and had absolutely no interest in being a part of it. I covered the details of this experience in my memoir; suffice to relate here that I didn't want any part of that platoon and tried to get back into the 3rd. After a few days of negative results from my requests and personal actions, a health issue caused me to be sent to the rear. When I returned to the company four days later, I was assigned to the 3rd Platoon. The company had received replacements from the States, and I could go anywhere I wanted. Motivation, yes!

Unfortunately some of us are not always fully motivated and involved with our team's mission and purpose. Many times we are simply rank-and-file fillers, moving forward because we have to. Isn't this a leadership problem? If each member of the team has not taken on the team's mission personally, then the leader has fallen short with his or her guidance. And what better way to get the team members directly involved than by causing them to feel that they have an important part to play? Letting them know they have a part to play doesn't begin and end with the plan's forward movement; team members must be involved at the planning stage if they are to be 100 percent motivated.

The leader has the final say on the game plan, but to the degree possible, the leader should ensure that each team member has a part in the makeup of that plan. Each team member should feel as though he or she is instrumental in accomplishing the objective. We all work better for those things and issues we believe in, those things of which we want to be a part. None of us are really motivated to simply follow the person in front of us and do what he or she wishes. We want and enjoy providing what it takes to accomplish the mission—and that is motivation.

Commitment

10

Leadership is the ability to recognize the special abilities and limitations of others, combined with the capacity to fit each one into the job where he will do his best.

J. Oswald Sanders, Spiritual Leadership: Principles of Excellence for Every Believer

Family and spousal commitments were addressed in chapter 3; here we take a closer look at the meaning of commitment as an essential element of leadership. Commitment, and all that the word means with regard to one's undertakings in achieving objectives and goals, involves many factors. There is the before, the during, and the follow-through involvement with all objectives and accomplishments. Before the commitment, for example, the leader must make the decision to start the planning phase, decide when to execute and work toward the objective, and be aware of the overall expense of the objective in material, people, and money.

Too much time spent in the decision process—how to accomplish a mission, its final objective, and whether or not to proceed with the mission—can be detrimental to the plan's purpose and objective. A late or slow start to a commitment can lead to failure because of changing circumstances. Some people in positions of leadership prepare incessantly; they want to make sure that all bases are covered, and in the process they can't commit to a start time. Many leaders wait until they have collected all available information regarding a mission before committing their team. Timing, however, is very important in most situations: Get on with it and adjust your plan as additional information becomes available. When all followers are committed to the team's objective, information continues to flow in all directions, inward, outward, downward, and upward.

We are all familiar with the saying "You can delegate your authority but not your responsibility." That is very true for the commander, for the leader, and for the president of organizations as well as our country. Those words really mean that the top leader can direct his subordinates to tackle and attempt to accomplish the mission; he gives them his authority to do so. But whether or not they are successful, the senior remains responsible to *his* leader. However, just as a senior leader gives authority to do whatever has to be done, he, that senior leader, can and should hold the junior leaders responsible to him for the actions taken or not taken. The leader remains responsible to his senior, but leaders at each level should hold their junior leaders responsible to them. This is commitment.

Marine leadership always had the personal touch of commitment throughout my years of service. Leaders at all levels were seen, out there with us, sweating and dying with the team. The actions of my mentor, Corporal Davis, made me aware of that important feature of leadership early in my career. Each of his actions stated loudly and clearly his commitment to his squad members. We mattered to him; he cared about us. He was involved with us and did for us in every way he could. Of course not all leaders rose to that standard; there were a few exceptions in that war. But we can't all be perfect. We can't all be a Corporal Myron Davis.

I observed much on the negative side of leadership with the U.S. Army in the Korean War. These incidents were not so much an individual commander's fault because the Army, overall, had gotten caught up short in preparation for that war, as had the Marine Corps. The Army found itself involved in another ground war when it was thought there would be no more such wars. Nevertheless troops on the ground suffered the consequences of those shortfalls. Army troops, both officer and enlisted, were trained only for occupational duty, which fell far short of the role of infantrymen in firefights in stopping the North Korean assault into the south.

The location of the leader plays a big part when involved with big issues, especially with situations that could easily cost one his life. Here I refer to the rifle platoon commander, the lieutenant in charge. Our Lieutenant Brimmer was always on the ridgeline crest, where he had eye contact with his squad positions maybe fifty to a hundred yards down from the crest. (Our fighting-hole positions were placed on what was known as the military crest of the ridge, which usually provided the defender with better fields of fire and was some distance down from the ridgeline crest.) Our platoon leader was with us, and he was involved with our every action, including providing supporting arms when and where we needed it.

During that war I was always unimpressed when we were relieved by an Army unit, usually an infantry battalion relieving our rifle company, and, as I usually did, heard the following question from an officer: "Where is your officer's tent set up?" These Army infantry company officers lived in tents on the back side of the ridge. They were down where they were safe from assault fire. How could they direct the fight when the enemy assaulted their defensive position? I suppose the squad leaders were set up on the ridge crest, leaving the riflemen forward in their fighting positions. Leadership was not placed and committed were it was needed, where it could be seen and felt.

I don't have personal knowledge on the following situations but have read about them over time, and I did hear much gossip along these lines among my buddies on our ridgelines in the Korean War. These words were supposedly spoken at different times by several higher Army commanders avoiding their leadership commitments (the me-first mentality) while under assault by enemy forces and about to be overrun. One regimental commander ordered, "Issue the grenades and every man for himself" as he got in his jeep and took off to the rear and safety. I understand that this type of situation took place several times in that war.

The Army had fighters who put up a good fight, and the Army had commanders who were good leaders and were committed to the mission with their troops, but on the negative side, there were just as many who were not prepared to fight, who only months prior had not expected to have to fight, and didn't have a problem with leaving it for someone else to do.

A Marine took the wrong approach in his handling of us, the members of his company. While what he did is also done by athletic coaches everywhere, especially football coaches, and this Marine major had no doubt played college football, I wasn't motivated by his manner because of his lack of personal commitment to our purpose. I was in a Marine Force Reconnaissance Company, and we all were in excellent physical shape. We recon Marines worked out daily with organized physical exercise and long unit runs (in addition to working out and running on our own). Our commanding officer was not always involved with us because he, no doubt, had commander issues to handle. My problem was that on the several times he did join us for an afternoon workout (he led the run), he was missing that sense of leader commitment.

The major's habit in leading the run was to have us line up on the sports field and sprint to him a hundred yards down the field on his command "Go." Then he would walk back to where we started while we lined up for another race. The major pointed out several Marines who were not trying very hard—"Do better; don't be last!"—and gave another "Go." I didn't like that approach; the sprints were good for me, but didn't the major need them too? We were hurting after a few sprints, but not the leader. This was a big reminder to me that my approach to leadership was a better one; I always did everything with my team, hurting and having fun, from the rank of corporal to colonel, and to me that is leader commitment.

Personal leader involvement is commitment, and personal commitment is very much a Marine Corps leadership element—an essential element. However, it is more evident today than in my early time in the Corps. Fifty years ago it was more the individual leader's choice as to his commitment to physical fitness training, and seldom did a leader himself run. For that matter very few if any Marine units or individuals had a run on their daily or even weekly schedule. In 1956 and 1957 I was the only drill instructor in the 1st Battalion, Marine Corps Recruit Depot, San Diego, who ran with his platoon of recruits. Running recruits at that time was for punishment; little running was done for physical fitness. The majority of drill instructors ran their platoons in a large circle around them as they stood in the middle of the drill field and barked commands: "You don't want to do close order drill, you don't want to march? Okay, we run!" Only the "we" was not in the run.

I liked to run my platoons through the sand down the back fence between the Marine Corps Base and the Convair airfield. This was not a workout run but punishment for not showing me what I wanted to see during our close order drill on the drill field. It was a good workout, nevertheless, and I usually would drop most of my recruits in the sand before I turned the platoon around for the return. I ran with them. For days after a run, all I had to do to get heels pounding the asphalt was say, "Maybe it's time for a run, screws!" (Sergeant Eakin over in the 3rd Battalion also ran with his recruits.)

My own Pathfinder and Force Reconnaissance leader positions were always conducted as a committed team member, regardless of my rank. I was involved in the hurting and sweating with the team, as I should have been. A unit's personnel physical condition agenda is the responsibility of the commanding officer, and that responsibility continues down to the lowest leadership billet.

In 1956 the Marine Corps established a physical fitness test, our Corps' first. It has changed and been called by different names over time, but the bottom line is that today the Corps ensures that Marines are physically fit to do the Marine thing. As a result of the physical fitness test, Marines have been motivated to run on their own in addition to the unit exercises, to get in shape, to do well on the test. This is individual commitment, but the commander is also committed to ensure that the agenda is carried out. My opinion is that personal involvement, the leader sweating and paining with the team, is the best way to do that.

The same company commander that liked to work us out with his run sprints conducted our company physical fitness test over a two-day period. The officers were tested on one day, and the enlisted Marines took the test on another (a "them and us" event). I didn't like that approach; something was missing, like maybe personal leader interest and commitment. Of course the major conducted the officer test, and the company officers conducted the enlisted test. Them and us.

My approach has always been that officers and enlisted Marines take the test together. Usually, because of duty commitments, all personnel can't be tested on the same day, but I never broke the test down to leaders and followers. The Marine way is that all ranks are tested together in all tests. That is everyday leadership, motivational commitment. I always took the test with my unit, detachment, platoon, company, and battalion.

There is team commitment as well as individual commitment, and I once was in a situation where these two, the team and the individual, were in conflict. This took place at Jacksonville Naval Air Station in Florida. It was 1963–65, my rank was acting gunnery sergeant, wearing the old technical sergeant chevrons, and I worked in the Marine Aviation Detachment's Operations Office. The operations officer was Captain Howard, and he also was the head of the detachment's rifle and pistol team. I became a team shooter.

Captain Howard's goal was to keep our pistol team qualification in the sharpshooter category, rather than move up to the expert level, so we would win more matches and bring home more trophies. He spoke very strongly on that point, and the eight of us on the team complied. It was easy for me at first because I was new at the National Rifle Association (NRA) type of match shooting. There is one big difference between this match and the Marine Corps pistol qualification course. That difference amounted to the fact that the NRA course was harder to master.

The Marine Corps pistol qualification course for the slow-fire match is, or was then, ten rounds, one at a time, with the targets on the twenty-five yard line. The NRA yardage for this ten-round, slow-fire match is fifty yards, and boy, does that make a difference. Because those .45-caliber pistol sights are so close together, if you are off a hair, in sight alignment or because of an improper trigger squeeze, you miss the entire target at fifty yards. Another major adjustment was required for the rapid-fire match: Marines fire at the fifteen-yard line and the NRA course does it at the twenty-five. That requires some hard, deep concentration on sight alignment and trigger squeeze to put ten rounds in the bull's-eye in ten seconds.

Because of the above reasons, I had no problem keeping my scores within the sharpshooter range during the early matches we attended. Working against that goal, however, was the fact that our office work was light and allowed us long lunch breaks. We would go to the pistol range daily at 1100 and bust caps (shoot our pistols) sometimes until 1400. We had plenty of ammo, and I got better with the pistol.

It got to the point where I had to "throw rounds away," as Captain Howard suggested. While that is good for the team's goal of keeping a low team qualification score, how does one do that and not affect his shooting ability, his individual commitment? In compliance I did as directed; I would get only nine rounds fired in the ten-round rapid-fire match. I also would sight in on the target at a different place rather than at the center of the bull's-eye, maybe six o'clock on the bull's-eye for one string and nine o'clock on another. That worked to keep my score down, but I didn't like it. I also wondered what it was doing for my shooting skill. Could I really get ten well-sighted rounds off in a rapid-fire match?

It came to a head for me later in that pistol team experience. There was a big pistol match going at Parris Island, South Carolina, over a weekend, and I was the only team member free to make it. I drove up and entered the match as an individual. These were NRA matches conducted by the Marine Corps Rifle and Pistol Clubs at both Quantico and Parris Island. Though I was aware of the need to keep my score down as I had been directed, it didn't happen. I fired all rounds in the rapid-fire matches, and even though I would take a sight focused at nine o'clock on the edge of the bull's-eye, many times all ten rounds would be in the black at nine o'clock in the bull's-eye. My intention was to aim at the edge of the black and get some five-point hits and some four pointers. I had no intention of sighting in on something other than the bull's-eye and getting twos and threes. (The target values are by rings, with the bull's-eye being five, the next ring four, and on down to two.) I had to have some fives to remain a sharpshooter.

Well, I didn't get enough fours. I had a tight wad of ten hits just in the black (the bull's-eye) in the nine o'clock position—too many times. I fired an expert score, and went home with an arm full of trophies. Captain Howard accepted it well enough; his only words were "Congratulations, wish I could have made that match." At this time all team members were shooting so well that we just had to move up, and we later brought home as many trophies as an expert team as we did as a sharpshooter team. The lesson is that commitment should suit both the individual and the team.

A problem for our Marines fighting the Vietnam War during my time was the lack of specific unit training and operational exercises conducted together as a team while not under fire. Missing for the new team members was the opportunity to discuss the hows, whens, and whys, as well as a good critique following the operations. We had this problem in the Korean War too, along with little to no infantry training as I addressed in an earlier chapter. All Marines sent to Vietnam were well trained in infantry tactics and well equipped. The problem was "individual replacement." At the beginning of the war and the initial commitments of combat units, Marines had trained and operated together as members of the team in the States, on Okinawa, or on Hawaii. They had experienced operations together and had opportunities to get to know their fellow team members. They knew what to expect of the Marines on their flanks and what was expected of them. Later in the war, combat casualties and completion of duty tours created the need for individual replacements into these units.

There are two basic ways to work replacements into active combat units. The best, which we did not do in either the Korean War or Vietnam War but are doing in the Iraq War, is pull the unit out of combat for an extended period of time. This gives the replacements a chance to learn their roles in their team's actions and to know their new unit's manner of conducting different operations while not under enemy fire. They can talk about it and critique their individual actions. The other way, individual replacement, places the individual Marine in a position vacated by a casualty or completion of a duty tour while the unit continues its combat mission. The replacement learns his role within the team and what is expected of him while his new unit conducts its operations on a day-to-day basis, many times under enemy fire.

A football analogy helps make my point. You can have eleven great individual football players who really know the game and have the required strengths and talents, but until a coach gets involved, teaches them the team plays, and has them practice and run their plays, they are not a winning team. They don't really know what is expected of them as individuals or what is expected of the other team members in any particular play.

I became aware of this shortcoming soon after taking command of Alpha Company, 1st Battalion, 9th Marine Regiment, 3rd Marine Division. We all were individual replacements in our assigned positions; we never had a chance to talk about or critique our actions in a noncombat environment. I learned that my rifle squads sent out on ambush missions were going to the proper trail junctions but instead of setting up their ambushes in accordance with Marine Corps tactics and as Marines were taught, they were forming a wagon wheel. This was a good all-around defense, but there was no kill zone as there was in a properly set ambush. Defense was not their mission, nor was it a concern, because the enemy did not or should not have known their location. I realized that this negative factor affected us in all of our different types of operations. We were deployed in combat, not in a training environment.

After about a month in command, I received the word to move my Alpha Company to Vandegrift Combat Base. My company would provide the base security for four days. This mission served two purposes: It provided ground security for the base and it gave the Marines of a rifle company a break from field operations. The routine was that the company's riflemen were all on the security/defensive perimeter line during darkness, but after an hour of daylight, 90 percent of the Marines could go into the base center for the day.

The center of the base was the living area for those assigned there and included squad tents with cots, mess tents, and a post exchange tent. My Marines ate hot chow, slept, visited the exchange, and received and wrote letters. This was a much-deserved rest and relaxation time, any way you cut it—four days of it.

Vandegrift Combat Base was a helicopter refueling and resupply area positioned out in the wild country with us, within our regimental operating area. Located in the western portion of I Corps, its birth took place during the Khe Sanh battles because it was not far from Khe Sanh. Choppers didn't have to fly far to get loaded with ammunition, weapons, water, and C-rations for delivery to the operating rifle companies. Refueling also was done there, saving many miles to the coast and the Quang Tri Marine Base as well as our Marine bases farther south at Danang. Vandegrift duty was a high point for the bush Marines (operating rifle companies), a great opportunity for rest and recreation. (Marines on the bases of Danang and Quang Tri considered Vandegrift in the bush—one could get killed there.)

I realized that I had a great opportunity to communicate with my Marines, to get inside their heads, during my company's first day at Vandegrift. I needed to talk with my warriors, talk about our shortcomings, what we could do better and how. My company gunnery sergeant was directed to have the company (minus the 10 percent manning the defensive line) on a bank of dirt behind our tents at 1400. At that time I moved down the wide path in front of the embankment before my standing Marines.

"Take a seat, Marines, I want to talk with you a little about our Marine business." After they were seated, and with a look of disgust on most of their faces because I was using up their personal time, I continued. "What is a good position or shape of a squad ambush? What is a good way to trigger an ambush?"

There were no responses and no hands going up. But I surely got the message that my plan and purpose weren't coming over well. The message on most of these young men's faces was "Class? School? Is this what this gungy SOB is up to? He's messing up my sleep time, my personal time with letters and a beer. This is my rest time." I nevertheless realized I needed to talk with my Marines and get inside their heads. Our bush operations and commitments demanded that we fix our shortfalls or we would pay a higher price in lives. I continued:

> Marines, we have a problem, and true, it is not ours alone because all Marine units are faced with the same issue. Individual replacement is the problem. Hell, you are all well trained infantry warriors, you know how to fight, to take the objective and defend it. Our problem is that we have never done this thing together. We have never assaulted an objective or defended one that allowed us to critique our individual efforts afterward—or for that matter, we have never talked about how we are going to do the mission beforehand. Seldom do we have a chance to talk about our operational commitments; we are in combat. Example: In your infantry training school you were taught to set up an L-shaped ambush with the kill zone centered on the trail intersection. How many of you here have used the L shape in your ambushes?

There were no show of hands and still plenty of sullen looks in the group. I went on:

> We have never trained or rehearsed, or had the opportunity to do any operations together where we could talk about what we were going to do and how we were going to do it, up to now. You don't really know what to expect from the Marine on your flank during any particular operation, and he doesn't know what to expect from you. Individual replacement is our culprit, and

we have an opportunity to rectify that shortcoming. What I'm really talking about, Marines, is providing each of us with the insurance that we go home on the Freedom Bird rather than in a body bag. You are only going to be out here for two hours each day we are here; this is your rest time and you deserve it. I want you to rest, but I also want you to stay alive. I want you on that Freedom Bird bound for your home and family when your time comes.

My football analogy followed, and I began to see a different facial message coming from my Marines. I continued with my talk on setting up an ambush: "1st Squad, 1st Platoon come forward." I directed the squad leader to set them up in an L-shaped ambush covering the trail junction, and I talked about what was taking place before them. "Where do we place the machine gun? The Claymore mine, how many? What position does the squad leader take? Who triggers the ambush?"

I had 1st Squad, 2nd Platoon come forward, move off to the flank, and come down the trail as the enemy and enter the kill zone. Who does what? When? I began getting some good contributions from my seated Marines. I was communicating with them and them with me. Next I had a friendly squad walk into an enemy ambush. Who does what, when? We all got so involved with our purpose and what we were doing that my two hours came and went with no one aware of it. I had individual and team commitment.

A couple hours every afternoon during our several assignments at Vandegrift were spent in this way, including assaults on fortified positions and discussion on defensive position setups. What really pleased me was later observing my squad leaders working new replacements into their role within their squad activities in the same manner. These squad leader classes were not necessarily done on Vandegrift, but wherever the leader was and whenever he had the time, no enemy threat, and the space. It was commitment within the squad, the team.

The requirement for leader commitment is not only on the individual and unit level but also on the level of the total force. Command involvement is exercising the meaning of the word "care," and it is about the commitment of all personnel, followers, and leaders in a fair and equal manner. During the Vietnam War officers in both the Army and Marine Corps were assigned to an infantry battalion for only six months. Then they would receive a staff job within a headquarters command somewhere in a safer environment. There were several justifications for this routine, one being to give more officers, including other than infantry military occupational specialties, combat command time and experience with rifle companies and platoons. For example, when I took over Alpha Company, one of my second lieutenant rifle platoon commanders had a motor transport military occupational specialty and another one was in communications. A second reason probably was that lieutenants, good rifle platoon leaders, didn't last long in a firefight.

There was a major negative side to this policy that I feel was overlooked and important to the force overall. As this order only applied to officers, it enforced the "them and us" mentality, which is never a good situation within a team. Enlisted Marines had to spend their entire thirteen months (later reduced to twelve) in a rifle company out in the bush—if they lasted that long.

This issue really hit home with me on several occasions when a young Marine would approach me with a request that he be assigned to one of our company supply or administrative jobs at our base camp back at Quang Tri. He would have had twelve months in the bush with the company, and perhaps had been wounded (at least once), and he didn't feel good about his chances of getting through another month out here. He wanted a job in the rear to ensure that he would go home in one piece to be with his family again. He felt that he had done his share and his job.

Those requests really hit me hard and bothered me greatly because these were great young Marines and they had done their job outstandingly; they were Marine warriors. I appreciated where they were coming from, but there were only a handful of jobs at our company rear, and they already were filled by Marines who had been wounded and also had their time in the bush. I would respond to these Marines' requests with that fact and that there were no positions open. Invariably their responses were along the line of "It is not fair. You officers only have to spend six months out here, and we enlisted have to stay here until we are killed!" That issue bothered me intensely, but there was nothing I could do about it. With an order such as this, the words "commitment," "care," and "concern" are not shown and individual commitment is not evenly shared by those within the unit. This was another "them and us."

Colonel Don Myers addresses this issue in his book *Leadership Defined*, and his point is that the order contributed to more casualties among the followers—which also expresses the leaders' lack of care at all levels for those whom they are responsible. He writes, "That was an effort to relieve the commanders of their responsibility of knowing their men and looking out for their welfare. It also gave more officers the opportunity of leading troops in combat at the expense of the troops. The turmoil that this particular order created was not considered." Let's never do that again.

Peter F. Drucker echoes my point on commitment in his book *Managing the Non-Profit Organization: Principles and Practices*: "The leaders who work most effectively, it seems to me, never say 'I.' They don't think 'I,' they think 'We.' They think 'Team.' They understand their job is to be making the team function. They accept the responsibility and don't sidestep, but 'we' gets the credit. There is an identification (very often, quite unconscious) with the task and with the group. This is what creates trust, what enables you to get the task done."

Good leaders are committed to mission, followers, and our great country. Nothing worthwhile is easy to achieve, and this includes positions of leadership. Once a leader is accepted as a leader, he or she is on for the long haul.

Communication

11

> When you look around, you've got to ask: "Where have all the leaders gone? Where are the curious, creative communicators? Where are the people of character, courage, conviction, omnipotence, and common sense?"
>
> *Lee Iacocca,* Where Have All the Leaders Gone?

Communication is an essential element of leadership, and it works in many ways, through many means, and in many directions. Nothing takes place or happens in the best interest of the members of the team without communication. We, individuals as well as teams, have to talk with one another. We have to get the word on the mission, the support available, the information on who is involved, the objective, and many other important facts. Once the mission is under way, the team members must be kept abreast of all changes and any unexpected situations encountered. And when members of the team need help in any manner, someone has to hear them, to be aware of their situation. Today, fortunately, communication isn't carried by a rider on horseback. While my focus here is on the military, my statements apply to many situations and organizations, including government and business organizations. If we aren't talking, we aren't producing the product, we aren't moving toward the accomplishment of our objective in the best interest of all concerned.

Lack of proper communication caused my first big personal embarrassment shortly after taking command of Alpha Company. After several days with the assignment of fire-support base security, I received my first mission, which gave me my first chance to shine before my Marines, but it turned out to be a screwup. Alpha Company was to fly out by chopper, land in bad-guy country, and move up a ridgeline to where we would prepare and open a new fire-support base. This preparation included clearing trees so that a helicopter could bring in equipment and a bulldozer to flatten out the ridge for artillery gun emplacements. The guns, crews, ammo, and support equipment would be flown in by choppers when we had the base ready.

My map showed our objective ridge had steep sides, was high in elevation, and was very narrow at the top. All were reasons that Colonel Barrow, our regimental commander, had chosen this spot for a new fire-support base: It would be easily defended, and the gun battery personnel could handle their own security, freeing up another rifle company for bush work. Our battalion air officer designated the helicopter landing zone for our insert so all I had to do was follow my selected route on my map reconnaissance from the landing zone to the ridge position. There was only one lead-up ridge near our landing zone, and that ridge went right up to our objective. Good, I thought. This will be easy enough to do, straight ahead Marines.

Alpha Company was relieved of its fire-base security mission by an Army rifle company (it was an Army artillery battery on Fire Support Base Ann), and we moved to the landing zone for our chopper ride. While waiting for the choppers, a disciplinary problem required my attention; that had me tied up, and I missed a radio call. As we later boarded our choppers, my radio operator gave me a note with the message I had missed over the radio. The message changed the location of our landing zone. We were now to land west of our objective rather than on the spot designated earlier on the east side of the ridge. It made sense because it appeared that our walk up would be much shorter if we landed at the new spot. While airborne, I studied my map and picked out a new route to our objective: Walk east up a narrow feeder ridge instead of west.

Communication in that open, noisy CH-46 was difficult, so I decided that there was no reason to talk with the pilot. He knew where he was taking us and so did I . But as it turned out, I should have confirmed our landing zone with him. He landed us in the original zone, though at the time I didn't know that. One zone looks like another in the jungle, especially if one has never seen it before.

The choppers were airborne immediately following our debarkation. I didn't like the look of things on the ground; there was no ridge or mountain to our east as I had expected to see above the jungle foliage. Gathering my platoon commanders, I informed them that we had landed in a different zone than the one we had planned to land in and that I had just gotten the word about the new landing spot as we boarded the choppers. There was dense jungle around this small landing zone, which restricted my view of the nearby terrain, but I could see a high ridge to the west of us. I could see no ridge to the east of us as I should have been able to if we had landed in accordance with my latest guidance. It really looked to me like we had landed in the first landing zone. I needed to talk with someone; I needed to communicate.

I directed my radioman to raise battalion. I wanted to talk with the operations or air officer. There was no response to his call. Neither our artillery forward observer nor the air officer could raise anyone on their nets. The chopper pilots had left the area fast and we couldn't raise them either. None of our radios had contact with anyone. It appeared to me that the chopper pilots had not gotten notice of the landing zone change, but I couldn't be sure without seeing more terrain or talking with someone.

I decided to go with my last order first, the way Marines are taught. We would move east until we could see more high ground or make radio contact. We started humping, and after about two hours we hit a ridgeline running in a southward direction. That didn't fit with anything on my map in reference to our second landing zone, but I headed south. About this time my artillery forward observer made radio contact with his fire-direction center. "Have them fire a flare over our objective," I told him. I climbed a tree in order to have a clear view of the high ridgeline to our west that I suspected was our objective. Sure enough, it was. That artillery flare bust right over that high ridge and floated slowly down on its parachute. Damn.

The new lieutenant company commander was not looking very good at this point, and as I walked back through my company while turning it around, each Marine's face sent the same message. Two hours out plus two hours back placed us at our starting point. Worse, in addition to our normal combat gear, we were loaded with chain saws, fuel, and explosive material, all needed to clear the ridge for a chopper landing with more gear. My platoon leaders had not had a chance to inform their Marines of our supposedly changed landing zone, and at that moment, those Marines were negatively impressed with this dumb lieutenant who couldn't find his way around.

Darkness caught us just a little west of our actual landing zone. We set in for the night and made our objective easily enough on the following day. If only we had had the global position system in those days. A lensatic compass and an old, inaccurate map weren't much help, and neither was our communication system. Whoever had decided to change our landing zone had failed to pass that word to the pilots. That communication screwup hurt Alpha Company, the commander, and his warriors for a day, but we got over it.

Today's high-tech equipment and communications environment give the commander several ways to communicate, and because some of them are not by voice, he or she won't have that important eye contact. Nevertheless, if the commander has communicated directly with his followers at every opportunity, messages will come across as desired, favorable. It is all about knowing and believing in one's leader. One's feelings toward one's leader cannot be expressed any better than this: "I would follow him to the very gates of hell." That was how I felt about my squad leader in the Korean War and my battalion commander in the Vietnam War. Communication plays a big part in instilling and reinforcing this feeling.

It is important for your followers to feel that your purpose, objective, and desires are theirs. If we all want the same thing, we stand a good chance of achieving it, regardless of the difficulties encountered. Communication is what it is all about, and I exercised communication with seven hundred Marines while I was the commanding officer of 1st Battalion, 6th Marine Regiment, 2nd Marine Division at Camp Lejeune. We were on a six-month deployment to Okinawa (without our families, of course), a deployment that meant we were one of our country's forward-deployed ground forces in defense of our national freedom. We were one of the several forward-deployed ground combat forces ready at a moment's notice to do whatever had to be done, wherever, and against whomever.

There were several personnel issues that had to be addressed if my battalion on Okinawa was to be known to be as good as I knew it was. At stake were the options available in battalion deployments off the island, that is, doing worthwhile operations rather than sitting around watching the sand blow on the beach. As soon as we were settled in our barracks with all of our gear and were pretty much squared away at Camp Schwab, I gathered my battalion in the base theater. My objective was communicating with my Marines, and I wanted that communication to operate in two directions, from me to them and from them to me.

We had two issues facing us, and I wanted my Marines' thoughts on them because it had to be their decision if what I had in mind was to work. A mustache on the face of a Marine was the first issue. The 3rd Marine Division commanding general, Major General Robert E. Haebel, did not like mustaches on Marines; he was of the old Corps, and in the old Corps Marines didn't wear hair on their face. Thus the general's favored battalions would be those that were in line with his standards.

The Marine Corps' grooming standards allowed a neat, trimmed mustache, and some of my Marines had them, especially some of the staff noncommissioned officers and sergeants. The word came to us from Major Van Huss while we were still at Camp Lejeune to get rid of the mustaches before we arrived on

Okinawa because the commanding general didn't like them. Well, that didn't sit well with several of my Marines because the Marine Corps' dress and grooming regulations allowed mustaches. I never brought up the subject while we were in the states, but once we got on Okinawa, I had to take it on. Several Marines had made statements in my presence while still at Camp Lejeune and then on the way over that their mustache was not coming off because they were within Marine Corps regulations.

With all of my Marines seated in the camp theater, I hit the mustache issue:

> Our division commanding general doesn't like mustaches. Let's handle that issue this way. His best battalions are going to get the off-island operations. We know that. Our battalion is the best as we have just proven that point with our predeployment operations and evaluations back in the states. Will a few mustaches affect our status with the loss of operational deployments? Maybe. Is it worth the chance?
>
> Our wives and sweethearts are back in the States, they won't see us for six months. So what is the big issue with shaving off the mustache? If it is because the "business girl" out in the villa will charge you more money, I'll pay the difference. Let's shave off our mustaches before the general's welcome aboard visit with us in two days. If you do that, we will get the operational deployments off of this tiny island. You shave them off now, you can start your mustache growth in time so that you will have something on your face when we deploy home in six months. If we do this, our battalion will have much to gain and really nothing to lose.

I needed input as to whether my Marines were with me. I wasn't positive that I had gotten through to my mustached noncommissioned officer Marines. (Much earlier, I urged a vocal response from my Marines regarding their feelings and attitude toward any current situation. The word "attack," shouted three times, was their gung-ho response to my feeler questions. This response came about as the result of a less-than-supportive incident shortly after my taking command at Camp Lejeune. This story is related in my memoir.) I asked, "One-Six, what do you do best?" and got an immediate and very loud "Attack! Attack! Attack!"

My Marines were with me, and the next day all mustaches were gone. Communicating with my Marines was all it took. In the end it was their decision. Some of the staff noncommissioned officers may not have been completely swayed by my argument, but at this stage they recognized that the entire battalion of Marines, not just me or the general, would be against them if they didn't lose their mustaches. All of our Marines would blame them if we didn't get any decent operational deployments.

The second big issue facing us on Okinawa was individual disciplinary problems. I addressed this issue in chapter 6. It's all about care, which amounts to each Marine taking care of his buddy, looking after a fellow Marine. We do that in combat, in a firefight; we never leave a fellow Marine behind. My approach to this issue caused my Marines to accept it as their approach, and that was the way it was. No Marine was left behind, meaning not one of my Marines came to my attention with a disciplinary problem during our six months on Okee.

The payoff was that we went on two major operations in Korea, Japan, and the islands of Tinian and Guam. We didn't get two months total on the rock, Okinawa. All of this came our way because that is what my Marines wanted out of their six-month deployment. While I planted the idea and the desire, the bottom line was that my Marines took it on personally; it was their thought and their plan, it was what they wanted. I communicated with my followers.

Communication is an essential element of leadership, and it works both ways, up and down. Team members have to talk with one another, know what is in one another's minds regarding a situation. Here I have focused on the leader's personal guidance to his followers, but it should be remembered that followers and junior leaders also must have a clear line of communication upward.

Michael Useem covers the upward aspect of leadership well in his book *Leading Up*, and I recommend that all leaders who desire to go the distance read and study it. Regarding the lack of upward leadership by the top leaders on both sides in our Civil War, he notes, "Blinded by personal prejudice and trapped by overwhelming egos, McClellan and Johnston ultimately did a disservice not just to their own reputations but also to the separate nations that they had pledged their honor to serve." Useem explains the negative side of both of these leaders and their problem of informing their superiors of what was going on and what they, McClellan and Johnston, expected to do in reference to their situation and the employment of their forces:

> In contrast, Robert E. Lee had mastered the art of leading up and when called to replace Johnston in the middle of the Richmond defense, he turned the tide against the Union. In the summary of Civil War historian Douglas

Southall Freeman, General Lee was able to do so in part because he "understood the President thoroughly, and he employed his knowledge to remove misunderstandings and to assure cooperation." Neither petty nor vain, Lee held to four guiding principles that are as pertinent to corporate warfare today as they were to the War between the States:

1. Keep your superior well informed of what you have done, what you are doing, and what you plan to do.
2. Regardless of how you feel about your superiors, display a respect for their position.
3. Avoid petty quarrels with your superiors in which you may be right but from which your reputation will suffer.
4. Estimate your competitive advantage as precisely as possible, not only to avoid the twin dangers of overconfidence and overcautiousness, but also to sustain your superiors' confidence in your capacity for precise analysis.

Our "take care of your buddy" commitment during our deployment to Okinawa worked well. I also had another ace up my sleeve that helped to keep my Marines out of trouble. While this didn't involve communication directly, I credit it as another reason for our clean liberty log with no disciplinary problems. This was a hump, a long hike that was our Saturday routine while on Okinawa.

Physical fitness is up front with Marines, and I was always focused on it while leading One-Six. Marine infantry battalions sometimes have to hump many miles in little time and with heavy combat loads. I know. I have been there, done that (see my memoir). My battalion's physical fitness objective started at Camp Lejeune, and I continued it with a scheduled hike every Saturday we were on the island.

We left that island after six months doing thirty-mile humps with all of our combat gear on our backs. Due to the distance and the heat, we would leave Camp Schwab in the middle of Friday night. While this got us back at Camp Schwab in the afternoon, most Marines, and me for sure, didn't do anything other than pass out on our racks. There was little interest in or energy to find out what was going on out in the villas. We needed rest and sleep. So did most of my Marines, and that long hump worked in our team's best interest. We were communicating because we wanted no personnel problems. My Marines put all they had into those humps.

If the leader is not communicating directly with his followers, that leader cannot be sure that his intent, purpose, and goals are being received, let alone understood and carried out. We sometimes need the middle man, but when it comes to passing along one's desires to those involved, the doers, nothing beats face-to-face communication. Words, as we all know, can even have a different meaning depending on the attitude and manner of presentation by the speaker. Nothing beats eye contact with a steady gaze and the words "We will do it!" or "We will do it this way!" Leaders have to express their desires, lay it out the way it is going to be, and the best way to do that is with eyeball-to-eyeball communication.

FROM HOSTILITY TO HOSPITALITY

Some time ago my pastor gave a sermon that began with him saying he understood that 65 percent of the people in our society today are not pleased with the way things are in their lives. He went on to ask why. Is it because we have electricity, which gives us all of the comforts of life—hot meals, indoor plumbing, air conditioning in the summer, and heat in the winter? Is it because of the telephone communications we have, including the cell phone, which allows us to talk and receive calls anywhere? Is it because we have modern medical facilities and emergency crews that can take us quickly to a hospital to save our lives?

My pastor speculated that the dissatisfaction could be a result of the hostility between individuals in our society. He talked about the changes we needed to make in order to bring hospitality to our hearts and to our society. Thinking about the subject, I feel that our problem has more to do with the lack of good, positive leadership, and that starts with parental leadership, mom and dad communicating with their children. Children should be raised understanding our society's past, present, and future, and how they, the children, want to fit into this society. They should consider how they might influence the development of society, making it better for the majority of the people.

My opinion is that the change in the family today is at the core of our society's problems. Six decades ago, moms and dads were their children's leaders. Children learned right from wrong, and there was payback for the wrongs committed. Today many children do not have both parents in the home. One, usually the mother, is the only source of leadership, and because she often has to work long hours, there is a lack in communication with her children.

Many of our young people are sucked in by negative guidance from the bad crowd, those involved in drugs, alcohol, and all of the other problems we have in our communities. We as a nation must focus on and work to better that social path from childhood to responsible adult with a positive purpose in life. Communication is the way to accomplish this goal.

SECTION III

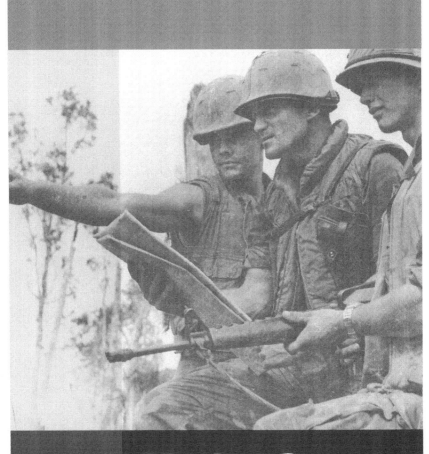

Marine Corps Combat Leadership

Personal Experiences and Viewpoints

12

There are only two kinds of people that understand Marines: Marines and the enemy. Everyone else has a second-hand opinion.

General William Thornson, U.S. Army

My memoir, *Marine Rifleman*, gives the details of my experiences in leading Marines, and most of those experience were good. I did, nevertheless, mess up a few times. The fourteen chapters of the memoir are titled by rank, private to colonel. At the end of each chapter I list the lessons I learned while in that particular rank with the idea that these lessons, especially the hard ones, might help today's young Marines and others involved in similar circumstances. In keeping with that thought, and the fact that most of the lessons I describe involve leadership, I list them here.

LESSONS LEARNED

As a Private

- Well-thought-out commitments, regardless of difficulty, are easily kept.
- Eleven weeks of boot camp makes a Marine for a lifetime.
- Discipline and heritage are the making of a Marine.
- Every person ought to experience a feeling similar to that of a Marine graduating from boot camp.

(The private first class and corporal lessons learned occurred during my combat tour of duty in the Korean War.)

As a Private First Class

- The spirit of a unit outweighs training in mission accomplishment two to one.
- Helping others gives us additional strength.
- Strength and endurance are factors of motivation.
- Marines should train with the weight loads they will later carry in battle.

As a Corporal

- Personal commitment in a firefight has to do with brotherhood and the Marine beside you more than Mom, apple pie, and the flag, all of which are far away.
- Combat is tough enough without removing a fighter from the bond of his unit and his friends.
- A tour of duty in a combat zone is one thing, a firefight is another.
- One man attacking at a time is a tough way to take an objective.
- A rifleman must know his rifle and his battle sights.
- Elite troops are wasted in the line when flank units cannot maintain their pace.
- Use and exercise all Troop Leading Steps.

As a Sergeant

- Integrity, dedication, and enthusiasm pave the road of leadership.
- Professionalism has a flavor; do all you can to improve the taste.
- Most young people do better if left alone to accomplish their assigned mission.

As a Staff Sergeant

- Spirited and well-meaning individuals also need checks and balances, someone on hand to say no.
- Seek followers with pride and commitment.

As a Technical Sergeant

- The stress caused by a beginner's early parachute jumps is not that different from the stress of a firefight in combat.
- Physically and mentally demanding experiences bond those who share them.
- A special uniform or device is not necessary to identify truly elite Marines or troops.
- The tougher and more demanding the training, the closer the bond between the individuals who share it.

As a Gunnery Sergeant

- Regardless of the barriers before you, if you want something strongly enough, continue to work hard for it.

As a Second Lieutenant

- You are never too old to start over.
- Seemingly superhuman tasks can be accomplished with a motivated team effort.

(First lieutenant and some captain lessons learned occurred during my combat tour of duty in the Vietnam War.)

As a First Lieutenant

- Some personalities and situations are not necessarily tailored to suit you: Zip up and give 100 percent; you will not be with any one person forever.
- Another man's war is difficult to conduct, especially in his manner.
- Positive leadership brings out the best in us.
- A winning team requires rehearsal and practice of the plays, even while involved in combat.
- Good ideas come up the chain of command as well as down.
- Body armor can cause casualties with a negative impact on mission accomplishment.

As a Captain

- Captain is the best rank of all in the Marine Corps.
- Capitalize on the abilities and initiative of squad leaders; give them responsibility.
- Instructor duty is the next best to field command.
- Evaluations are motivators when the evaluator himself competes in the evaluation.

As a Major

- Developing new ideas and a better means to accomplish an old task is interesting and exciting.
- Repetitive training causes near-instinctive reactions during life-threatening situations.

As a Lieutenant Colonel

- A battalion of Marines is not too large a unit for the commander to enjoy personal involvement in unit activities.
- When a commander communicates with his Marines, they will respond, give up, and do without in spite of the sacrifices to themselves—because the commander asked.

- If your billet or job can be dissolved upon your departure, maybe you ought to speed up the process.

As a Colonel

- Young people must select and shape their goals in accordance with their capabilities. In this instance, desire is rated less than 50 percent.
- The art of leading others is very important to our society, so why are there so few institutions of higher learning that offer a degree in something so important to the people?
- The ability to handle stress is key to combat leadership. Those who cannot function under life-threatening situations are not suited for the Marines.

COMBAT COMMANDS

I related in earlier chapters that Corporal Davis was my first leadership mentor. He also selected me to be one of his fire-team leaders, a corporal's position, while my rank was private first class and I'd only been eight months in the Marine Corps. Other than having to give up my Browning automatic rifle, I was pleased with the assignment. I was in charge of three Marines; we were a four-man fire team. Boy, did I have a lot to learn—and not just regarding leadership. I needed to learn how to survive while maintaining an acceptable personality and get the job done when my team members resented my placement over them as their leader.

The issue with two of my team members was that I was a boot Marine. The fourth Marine, my rifleman, was like me, eight months out of boot camp. The other two were activated Reservists, and though neither was old enough to have been in World War II, they had more time in the Marine Corps Reserves than I had in the Corps. The two pretty much talked down to me, and if they bothered at all to do what I directed them to do, they were slow in doing it. They clouded my early days in my new leader position to the point that I wondered if it was even worth it. But if I wasn't the leader, then it would have to be one of them, and I would have none of that. I worked hard at trying to make the difficult situation work.

Our platoon leader, Lieutenant Brimmer, promoted me to corporal about a month following my fire-team leader assignment. The promotion took place in April with a date of rank of 21 March 1951. My team members never used my rank when addressing me; it was always Fox this and Fox that. One day the old salts obviously were talking about me when I heard one of them state, "Just wait until he gets back in the States and he has to take a written test for corporal." The insinuation was that I would not pass a test of words; we all missed the fact that there is no better test to qualify one for a noncommissioned officer rank than leading Marines in actual combat.

All of the above took place during noncombat situations because we were not moving in the assault or under likely enemy action. We were just sitting on a ridgeline, with our battalion's assignment of regimental reserve, getting fat off of C-rations; all we had to do was eat, sleep, and bitch. However, once we moved out, the situation changed with my two disgruntled followers. I was now the one responsible, the one who had to call the shots. The two old salts were satisfied that all responsibility lay on my shoulders, not theirs.

The night of 19 May, Lieutenant Brimmer tasked me with manning a two-man listening post down a finger ridge from the one we had dug in on that day. This was the front line, the MLR we had just occupied that day. That listening post assignment required that both Marines on it were awake and listening for movement. When noise was heard, they were to move quickly back to the line and ensure everyone was up and ready for the enemy assault.

My rifleman, Baker, and I had the first half of the night on the listening post; my Browning automatic rifleman and his assistant had the last half. I had given them their choice of time on the post. Our sleeping time, the other half of the night, was done in our positions on the line. At 0200 the first watch was over. Leaving Baker in the listening post position, I returned to our line to wake our relief. As they were about to move out down the ridge, my rifleman appeared out of the darkness.

"What are you doing here?" I asked.

Baker responded with, "Hell, I ain't staying out there by myself."

"I gave you your choice and you didn't want to come up here and wake our relief, either."

The Browning automatic rifleman chimed in: "I ain't going out there when I don't know where the position is in the dark and if the enemy is already on it." His assistant sounded off in support: "We're not going out there."

I told Baker to take them out to the position, and he responded that he could not find it in the dark. There was nothing left but for the boot corporal to take the Browning automatic rifle team to the listening post. My manner in doing so was not smart; I crashed through the bushes going down the hill. The boot corporal was mad. He was also very lucky that the Chinese movement forward had not happened at this point. He would not have survived. I got the Browning automatic team on the position and I returned to the line for my sleep. That didn't happen. I got less than an hour in my sleeping bag because a Chinese army battalion walked up that ridge and hit us—but my listening post had us awake and ready.

My squad engaged in a major battle for the remainder of that early morning of 20 May, against a much larger Chinese Army force. As Corporal Davis was no longer with us, there were no noticeable leadership actions within our 3rd Squad that would serve my purpose with this book. Earlier I covered the fact that Estel Tuggle was severely wounded by a Chinese grenade; that happened in this fight, and the complete battle story is told in my memoir. Thanks to our listening post mission, however, our platoon suffered only two Marines killed and one seriously wounded compared to the Chinese loss of 152 killed and fifteen prisoners taken. That Chinese unit was obviously short on real leadership—thank goodness. Our platoon owes a debt of gratitude to Lieutenant Brimmer for sending out that listening post that night. Without it, the casualty count would not have been in our favor.

The Chinese battalion was also short on intelligence. The prisoners' response to the interrogators' questions were that they didn't know the "cloth tops and canvas legs"—referring to our camouflaged helmet covers and canvas leggings, which only Marines wore in those days—were on the hill. (Our battalion had moved in to replace the Army regiment maintaining that section of the front line on the nineteenth, only there was no unit on the line to replace. The Army personnel, individually, had bugged out. I also cover this story in my memoir.) The Chinese force expected the U.S. Army to be there, and they knew the U.S. soldiers would move to the rear as they, the Chinese, moved up the hill. They didn't expect to fight, which was the reason there was no assault fire. They just walked up the ridge. The prisoners stated that if they had known the cloth tops and canvas legs were on the hill, they would never have moved forward.

As a result of this information on the enemy's read-out of the forces against them, Marines were later issued army boots and we no longer wore leggings. Also, Army personnel began wearing camouflage helmet covers, which had been solely a Marine item of uniform throughout World War II and up to this point. Anything to confuse the enemy. For a while the Communist forces must have been impressed with how fast the Marine Corps had grown in personnel strength.

DRILL INSTRUCTOR

Setting a good example is and always has been a big part of leadership in the Marine Corps. My experiences as a drill instructor on the drill field at the Marine Corps Recruit Depot at San Diego in 1955 placed me face to face with the issue of setting an example in regard to personal appearance, duty performance, and individual conduct. This was a year before Staff Sergeant Matthew C. McKeon drowned six of his recruits in the Ribbon Creek incident at Parris Island, South Carolina. Up until the McKeon incident, drill instructors had a free hand; we did pretty much what we wanted to do and whenever we wanted to do it with our recruits. There was never anyone around to say no, don't do that; there was no one looking over our shoulders. Because of this lack of upper-level leadership, including the "command" atmosphere, something like the Ribbon Creek incident, or even worse, was bound to have happened.

We had no uniform that identified us as drill instructors; we all wore utilities with the utility cover. All drill instructors wore pistol belts (as did all personnel on official duty anywhere), and the senior drill instructor wore a .45-caliber pistol holster (empty) on his belt, but that was it. Most drill instructors wore the same set of utilities day after day, or at least they looked like it because few ever pressed their utilities. Most would crap out in their duty hut on their sleeping rack during the day while their platoon of recruits attended classroom instruction. They would rise, get their platoon, and go about their business looking just the way they did when they got up. I and a very few others didn't follow that route. I pressed my uniform each night and never lay down in it. I wanted to impress my recruits with the importance of looking like a Marine, and that included setting the good example, always.

Performance of duty was often in the same sad state: Do what you want when you want to do it. I covered earlier how many drill instructors ran their platoon of recruits around them in a large circle while they stood in the center and barked commands. This of course was done for a disciplinary reason, but that was the drill instructors' attitude: them and us. We held reveille on our recruits as early as 0400 in order to get them in and out of the chow hall in time to meet our training schedule; no one ever followed the chow hall schedule, if there was one. Do as you want.

Individual drill instructor conduct was also more or less a free enterprise. Many drill instructors' behavior went far below what is acceptable in a humane society. Depending upon a recruit's violation (sneaking a cigarette smoke was a biggie), we all awarded punishment that would be unacceptable in today's Marine Corps.

McKeon caused the change in the way Marines are made, and this change involved positive leadership. As a result of his screwup, my last year as a drill instructor was conducted on a written schedule, under direct observation of a technical sergeant and a captain. I did very little on my own, and there was absolutely no recruit harassment or punishment, verbally or physically. The manner of making Marines has changed, but the end product is every bit as good as it ever was.

RIFLE COMPANY COMMANDER

My next combat leadership privilege was as a rifle company commander in the Vietnam War. Though I was a first lieutenant in that war and the Marine Corps' Table of Organization lists rifle company commanders as captains, my unit check-in and statement of my desired duty assignment as a rifle company commander was not unique. Then as now it all has to do with the needs of the Marine Corps and the situation. There have been times that corporals were company commanders until replacements could reach the company following a firefight. In my case, my permanent rank at that time was first sergeant; my officer commission was temporary.

I had done my one-year tour in Vietnam as an advisor to an infantry battalion in the Vietnamese Marine Corps and had extended my tour in Vietnam for six months. My plan was to do the six months with my Marines up in the I Corps Tactical Zone, the northernmost position in what was known then as South Vietnam. Even thought my rank was lieutenant, I hoped to luck out with command of a rifle company; if not that, then I wanted assignment to one of the two in-country Force Reconnaissance companies.

The 3rd Marine Division personnel officer assigned me to the 1st Battalion, 9th Marine Regiment with the following statement: "I'm sure you can get a rifle company in One-Nine, hell, a corporal was a company commander for a while last year. Officers don't last long in that battalion. Have you never heard of the 'Walking Dead'?" I wanted to reply, "They're Marines; a better name for the battalion is 'Walking Death.'"

A chopper ride delivered me to Fire Support Base Ann, where 1st Battalion Headquarters was set up along with one rifle company, Alpha, providing security for the fire-support base. The other three rifle companies were patrolling within their separate assigned areas nearby. I was escorted to the tent of the battalion commander, Lieutenant Colonel George W. Smith. He would be the one to assign my duties, and with his question as to my preference of duty, I replied, "Command of a rifle company, Sir!"

We talked for about an hour, the colonel learning about me and me learning about his battalion (I covered this interview in chapter 5). One-nine had been involved in most of the bigger battles taking place in northern I Corps, Con Thien and Khe Sanh to name two. I was very much impressed with my new leader: He had that Marine look, he was serious yet friendly, and his focus and interest were his Marines. It was his intent in our conversation to make sure that I filled the bill concerning his requirements for a leader of one of his rifle companies. He gave me Alpha, the company there on the fire-support base with him.

January 1969 found the Walking Death Battalion out in the Khe Sanh area looking for the bad guys. The entire Khe Sanh area was divided into four tactical areas of operations, and our four rifle companies set up and worked company patrol bases. But no enemy forces were found. We had no significant enemy contact during the two months I was in the battalion, and as we also found none in the vicinity of or on Khe Sanh, I was satisfied that the war was over. However, there was one more area where we might find enemy forces.

Following our Khe Sanh operation, we started focusing on an operation into the A Shau Valley, which was home turf to the North Vietnamese Army forces. This valley was along the Vietnam-Laos border and included the Ho Chi Minh trail. Our operation was named Dewey Canyon and involved the entire 9th Marine Regiment. Other battalions also got involved before it was over.

OPERATION DEWEY CANYON

Some of our Dewey Canyon operational situations, especially the involvement of other Marine leaders, are covered in other chapters. Here I relate some of my personal experiences on that operation as a member of the team, Alpha Company. No two ways about it, the company commander has an easier role than a rifleman in a combat environment. As I was always somewhere near the center of my company perimeter, I didn't have to dig as deep a fighting hole as my Marines on the line. I had to dig out a hole something like six feet long, two feet wide, and about two feet deep—deep enough to place my body below ground surface. But that is a lot of digging if there are rocks, and the A Shau ridges had their share. Several nights, though, due to the enemy situation, I did dig a deep fighting hole, even though I was in the center of my perimeter or in our company section of a larger perimeter.

The night Major D. N. Kennon was killed is a good example of when I had to dig a deeper hole. We had jumped off on Operation Dewey Canyon, and Charlie Company was in the lead of our two-company assault along the ridgeline to the Laotian border. We had Headquarters and Service Company with the battalion command group between us on that ridge. (Bravo and Delta Companies were attacking south on the ridgeline to our right and in the same direction.) Charlie Company walked into an effective enemy defense, meaning that the enemy was set up on the far side of a cut through our ridgeline providing the enemy with a near-perfect field of fire. (A cut looks as though a bulldozer has cut and pushed tons of dirt over the sides of a ridge.) The cut was maybe fifty yards distance front to rear, and left to right at the bottom of the cut. The cut was forty to fifty feet deep, and the bottom, or floor, was clear of vegetation. The drop down in the cut and the climb up the other side were steep but manageable by foot-mobile, combat-loaded Marines.

The North Vietnamese force on the far side of the cut and looking down into it waited until Charlie's assault platoon was entirely in the cut before they opened fire. Charlie took many casualties before Captain Jack Kelly could bring effective fire on the enemy force. He did, and he recovered the Charlie casualties who needed to be medevaced out, both dead and wounded. It was late in the evening, so our battalion commander, Lieutenant Colonel Smith, elected to hold up where we were, set up for the night, and get the casualties out the next morning. Trees and brush had to be cleared to make a helicopter landing zone within our perimeter. Charlie Company formed the forward half of our defensive perimeter, Headquarters and Service Company set up in the center, and I moved Alpha Company up to tie in with Charlie for the other half of the perimeter.

Darkness fell as I gave guidance to my platoon leaders regarding our upcoming night activities: "Have your men dig deep fighting holes. I feel we'll see more of these bad guys tonight." Though I was in the center, I dug a deep fighting hole, electing to sleep sitting up in that hole. I didn't have a good feeling about that night; I expected the worst, meaning I was sure the North Vietnamese Army would hit us again. I checked my line in the dark and was satisfied that we had done all we could in the time we had. Our fields of fire were not good due to the jungle growth, but it was dark before we had a chance to clear them. This vegetation also allowed the enemy force to be on us before we knew they were there. I had each platoon commander place a listening post forward of his area, thought they were not out very far.

All hell broke loose in the middle of the night. We were under heavy automatic-weapons fire, which included several machine guns that swept our three-company position just above ground level. Mortar rounds and rocket-propelled grenades were also striking inside our perimeter. The fire was coming from Charlie Company's side of the perimeter; there appeared to be no assault force threat into Alpha's line. However, the incoming fire covered us well, and I was extremely grateful that my Marines were well under ground. Alpha Company suffered no casualties from that assault.

The enemy force had returned to the edge of the cut where they had been earlier when they hit Charlie Company. From that position they threw the stuff at us, but they never did a ground assault. Charlie Company returned fire, and our artillery-placed "danger close" and mortar fire obviously discouraged further action.

Charlie Company and Headquarters and Service Company took a number of casualties from the enemy fire, and the fact that many within Headquarters and Service Company were not sleeping below ground-surface level added to our loss. Our battalion operations officer, Major D. N. Kennon, was killed as he moved to his operations radio operator from his sleeping position to get him involved in repulsing the enemy fire. Now we really needed medevac helicopters, and it would be late the following day before we got all of the dead and wounded out.

Captain George Meerdink Jr., the company commander of Bravo Company, was killed on 22 February 1969. He had just moved his company down the Ho Chi Minh trail to the position I held until Colonel Smith assigned me another mission. Earlier, Meerdink and Captain Riley's mission had included attacking down the ridgeline to the west of us until they hit the Laotian border. On the twenty-first, Riley's Delta Company, after hitting the border, had proceeded east to Lang Ha-Bn, leaving Bravo on their ridge junction with Laos. Delta Company arrived just as my company was leaving Lang Ha-Bn. Likewise on the twenty-second, as Delta Company moved out to help my company, Bravo Company arrived on Lang Ha-Bn and occupied the positions vacated by Delta.

The North Vietnamese had mortared our hilltop at Lang Ha-Bn, which also was identified as our Objective Foxtrot, shortly after Alpha Company had occupied it following our assault on the twentieth. It was not heavily defended, and as their troops withdrew, they mortared us. They missed us; all their rounds fell on the hillside below. But their forward observer obviously made the necessary corrections to get rounds on his target because Bravo Company received mortar rounds shortly after its arrival on Foxtrot and the departure of Delta Company.

His Marines were under cover and Captain Meerdink and his command group were in a bunker on that hill. Because he was the kind of leader who stepped forward and did something, Captain Meerdink, along with his artillery forward observer, a lieutenant, decided to move outside of the bunker to get a good compass azimuth on the popping sounds of the enemy's mortar tubes. (They would follow with bringing in counterbattery fire on that position.) But that act of leadership did not work in the best interest of Bravo Company or, for that matter, our battalion. An enemy mortar round hit and exploded right beside the two officers, killing both of them instantly.

My mission on 22 February 1969 was to determine if the enemy unit located the day before by my 3rd Platoon, commanded by Lieutenant Bill Christman, was still in its position and, if it was, to do something about it. (I cover Lieutenant Christman's action in the next chapter.) Because of the dense jungle and my movement, I couldn't use my 60-mm mortars, so I left them on the ridge with battalion headquarters and Charlie Company. This meant that I had fewer than ninety Marines looking for a fight. My strength became smaller as my point squad was hit by what turned out to be an enemy outpost, costing me one killed in action and one seriously wounded.

I initially had Lieutenant Christman guiding my assault platoon to his place of contact with the enemy the day before. As it turned out, Christman selected the wrong path at a trail junction, and that caused us to pass about five hundred meters to the flank of the enemy force. Their outpost was on the creek bank and to the right rear of the enemy force in reference to our approach. When we hit the outpost, we had bypassed the enemy force.

The action at their outpost naturally alerted the enemy force, but they were slow with their response. As there appeared to be no further action, I radioed battalion to send down their water detail as planned; we were at the creek with no further enemy action. Headquarters and Service Company and Charlie Company Marines were out of water because low clouds and rain had prevented any chopper resupply.

After about half an hour, the water detail arrived, and as they filled their canteens, the enemy opened up with a machine gun and a mortar. Because of the distance between the enemy position and us, and the thick jungle growth, their fire was ineffective. The machine-gun tracers and bullets were flying through the trees high above us but really didn't come across as a threat. The mortar rounds also detonated high in the treetops and didn't hurt anyone in my company. A couple members of Charlie Company's water detail were hit by some small shrapnel from the tree burst over the creek. I had to commit a rifle squad to carry my two earlier casualties and to take the leaderless Charlie Company water detail back up the ridge to battalion and Charlie. Alpha Company was now minus a total of ten warriors from my earlier count of ninety.

The enemy fire gave me a direction for my assault. I now knew where the North Vietnamese unit was located. Shortly after arriving at the creek, Lieutenant Christman approached me with the fact that he had selected the wrong trail at an intersection and that the active machine gun appeared to be in the position that he had encountered the day before. The enemy force was now to our right rear. I moved two rifle platoons in the assault toward the source of the weapons fire, followed closely by my command group and my rifle platoon in reserve, the 2nd Platoon.

Our forward movement slowed as we neared the enemy position, and their fire increased, with multiple machine guns. We closed on the enemy defense, but their weapons fire was so heavy that my assault stalled; Alpha Company came to a halt. Because of the foliage, I couldn't fully determine what was happening, who was doing what, and what needed to be done.

Inspirational leadership, or at least the out-front-type leadership, didn't fit in this situation because of the dense jungle growth. A leader could directly influence only two Marines at a time, the one on his right and the one on his left, because he was not visible to the other members of his unit. I learned this quickly after my assault stalled, and I realized that the enemy force was stronger than I had expected. This North Vietnamese army unit no doubt outnumbered my Marines by a good amount, judging by their heavy fire. It sounded like they had a machine gun firing at each and every one of my warriors.

I had to determine our next action. What could I do to get our assault moving forward again? I had to move along my assault line because I couldn't raise either of my two assault platoon leaders on my radio. I would learn later that both, Second Lieutenant William J. Christman III and Second Lieutenant George Malone, had been severely wounded at this early stage in our fight. What was happening to my Marines in the assault?

Telling my radio operators and command group, small as it was, to hold this position and I would be right back, I moved forward in the thick vegetation. My assault Marines were only thirty yards or so forward, and I would make quick contact. The first Marine I encountered had been cut down by machine-gun fire, killed in action. I moved to the right of him because I saw another uniform lying on the ground. This Marine had been wounded by gunfire and was unconscious; just to his right a corpsman was tending to another wounded warrior. There was plenty of gunfire on all sides of me, so I knew we were still in the fight. Continuing my movement along our line, I hoped to get a solid feel for our situation and what I could do to get our assault moving.

Another Marine's body came into my view just as a rifle round whizzed by my head and a rifle report sounded in a tree to my front. I realized that a North Vietnamese soldier was in that tree and he had killed the Marine before me, and at the same time I saw the Marine's rifle lying there by him. I dove for the rifle, picked it up, and quickly determined that it was loaded and off safe. I was ready for the enemy soldier when he looked around the tree at me. My first round got him, but as he slouched around the tree in my direction, I made sure he was taken care of with a couple more rounds. He had secured himself in the tree with a rope.

Company commanders are armed with pistols because they are not normally directly involved in firefights. The pistol is for personal protection, and because I thought the enemy force was forward of my assault line and me, I had not taken my pistol out of my holster. A rifle was a better tool for handling the sniper, anyway. I hung on to that M-16 rifle a little longer.

Marines were firing forward of me as I continued moving to the right along my line, and I could see some of their action, though it was all on the ground and in thick vegetation. Our situation did not impress me favorably, and I thought Alpha Company was hurt worse than it actually was at that moment. If a Marine on the ground was not firing his rifle, he appeared as another casualty to me. Thinking on our situation, I felt that I had two options: break contact and withdraw or commit my 2nd Rifle Platoon, which I held in reserve.

My preference was to break contact, but that meant that I had to be sure I had all of my Marines and corpsmen, and how could I be positive of that in that thick stuff? With the heavy enemy machine-gun fire, one couldn't walk around and check the bushes. I would lose more Marines getting our casualties out from under the enemy's guns. And would I have enough Marines to carry our dead and wounded and fight off the enemy at the same time? I had fewer than eighty Marines going into the fight, and at this point I believed half of them were casualties.

My decision was the second option: commit my reserve. But would fewer than twenty Marines make a difference? I had committed a squad from the 2nd Platoon on the earlier mission that day, plus they had the two casualties suffered when we hit the enemy outpost on our way down the ridge. All Lieutenant Jim Davis had to take forward were two understrength Marine rifle squads. That was my decision, however, and I made it because I knew we would either walk out of this valley or stay in it forever.

It worked. My 2nd Platoon, after much fighting, made the difference. I cover in the next chapter the actions of my executive officer, First Lieutenant Lee Roy Herron, in leading the 2nd Platoon forward after Lieutenant Davis, along with the rest of my command group, was wounded by a mortar round.

All of my radio operators were down and out of the fight from the mortar round explosion among us. As I tried to move with three radios, Lance Corporal Mike Winter, one of my snipers, moved up and took one radio. Together we moved forward to a depression in the ground that offered some protection from the grazing machine-gun fire. We were raked over by that fire, and Mike caught a round in his leg and was out of the fight. (I describe my awareness of the loss in leader effectiveness and my fear during the time I was pinned down in my second book, *Courage and Fear*.) That was the low point in the fight for me because there was at least one more machine gun to knock out, and it was placing fire only inches over me.

After a while the sky cleared above us and I realized I could work and control air support. I called Colonel Smith and learned that he had two OV-10 aircraft on station in case I needed them. I directed the pilots onto the last machine gun, and that finished our fight.

All Alpha Marines didn't walk out of that valley, but those that couldn't were walked out by Alpha and Delta Company Marines carrying them in poncho litters. This was purely a rifleman's fight, right up to the last few minutes. Artillery couldn't be used as we were locked into the enemy when we located them; we were too close. Another problem was exact ground location, a difficult task in that jungle with a lensatic compass and a map that was usually off by a thousand yards or so regarding terrain features, which you couldn't see anyway in that jungle. The rain and low clouds made air support only a dream until later, when I was able to bring in the two OV-10s for the final knockout punch.

I covered in an earlier chapter what gave Alpha Company the ability to win that fight even though we were outnumbered, outgunned, and outpositioned. What I mean by outpositioned is that the North Vietnamese were in prepared, dug-in defensive positions: underground bunkers with machine guns and planned fields of fire. Though I didn't approach the enemy position in the direction that was expected and for which they were primarily prepared, the enemy adjusted quickly enough. Alpha Company was the aggressor in the assault, meaning on top of the ground and moving. A three-to-one ratio is preferred for an assault unit compared to a dug-in defense. Numbers tell the tale in this fight. The facts are that there were 105 enemy soldiers killed in that fight and I had fewer than 80 Marines going into it.

My Marines and corpsmen were the reason we overcame the bigger enemy force, and I feel strongly that our tactics classes at Vandegrift Combat Base were instrumental in our victory. My Marines knew what to expect from me, what was going on in my mind, as well as in the mind of his buddy on his flank, and they knew what was expected of them. Though all of my platoon leaders were out of the fight, my platoon sergeants, squad leaders, and fire-team leaders stepped forward with the leadership needed to overcome the enemy force. Individually and as a team, my gunfighters continued to move to the sounds of the enemy's guns. That was our duty, our purpose for being in uniform and for being in that valley.

Twelve of my Marines were killed that day, eleven in that action, plus one at the outpost encounter. Fifty-four of my Marines had to be medevaced out the following day due to a threat of loss of life or limb. The remainder, almost to a man, were wounded but chose to remain out there with the team, our company on Operation Dewey Canyon. I cover Captain Riley's Delta Company arrival to assist us that day in the following chapter.

As I wrote this, I referred to the green memoranda pocket notebook I carried on that operation for some of the information I provided above and was reminded of much that I had forgotten. For example, I had forgotten Alpha Company's total casualty count for the entire Dewey Canyon operation. From my company's commitment on 11 February (which followed our assignment as firebase security on 20 January to 10 February) until our lift-out on 18 March, we suffered 24 Marines killed in action and 129 wounded in action. Of that number of wounded, 89 were medevaced because of the threat of loss of life or limb. The forty Marines and corpsmen with less severe wounds stayed in the bush, in action with the team. I also received replacement Marines several times.

These numbers, however, don't tell the complete story because some Marines were wounded in one action, stayed with the company, and were wounded again or killed in a later contact. Lieutenant Bill Christman was one of the Marines in this category. He was wounded early in the operation and killed days later. A second point is that these numbers were from a rifle company that never had more than 150 boots on the ground on any one day. Many days my company strength was far under 100, especially after 22 February, but we were Marines with a job to do.

Marine commanders, beginning with the rifle platoon leader, will always be found forward with the action. That is the way they are taught at the Basic School, that is what they expect to do, and that is what is expected of them by their Marines. That is also why the Marine Corps uses a lot of lieutenants during wars. Though for the majority the role of rifle platoon leader is their choice, their first choice, it is a very demanding leadership position. It is also very high on an evaluator's list of commendable positions of leadership.

Leaders on My Flank

13

> I have only two men out of my company and twenty
> out of some other company. We need support, but it is
> almost suicide to try to get it here as we are swept
> by machine-gun fire and a constant barrage is on us.
> I have no one on my left and only a few on my right.
> I will hold.
>
> *First Lieutenant Clifton B. Cates, 19 July 1918*

S ince putting on the Marine uniform in 1950, I have been impressed with Marines' dedication to one another, their unit, the Corps, and our country. There are so many individuals who belong in this final chapter that I wondered whether I should write it. How could I write about only a few Marines and pass over so many who also deserve a place in this chapter? There were always Marines on my flanks, and they were leaders in whom I had the fullest confidence. Nevertheless I will single out a few of these great Americans, members of the Marine team. These Marines were gunfighters in the fullest sense and meaning of the word. They are covered in my memoir to a degree, but here I tell their full stories.

Before I cover their stories, however, I'll quote Gene Duncan's words on America's sons who become Marines for life. Major Gene Duncan, USMC (Ret.) has written several great books about Marines, and because he has been in the trenches, he has an in-depth understanding of what Marines are all about. His words, from his unpublished book "The Bugle Echoes Still," clearly define a Marine's purpose and mental makeup:

There is forever a place in the world of wolves for the Gunfighter. He is America's son. He answers her call and goes on to remain at the ramparts for the bulk of his years. He gives of himself unselfishly and totally.

To support and defend the Constitution of the United States against all enemies, foreign and domestic. Those are the simple guidelines which cause him to suffer privation, injury, frustration, grief, and ingratitude from the fickle protected. And yet, he knows honor as only a Marine Gunfighter can know it, and that seems to him to be the most important part of living.

Intolerant of incompetence and sub-standard performance and conduct, he demands from others what he gives to them, dedication, loyalty, excellence, and a fierce determination to defend his country and his Corps from all enemies, foreign and domestic. And in times of peace, it seems the enemies are mostly domestic.

Even in view of the mistaken premise that today's Marine must be a diplomat as well as a warrior, our Gunfighters—those fierce, no-nonsense centurions—are the ones who come forward when the battle is joined, while the diplomats seek shelter *from what they have created,* and who will, when the smoke has cleared, denigrate their saviors and place them back in a position of inconsequence.

But the heart of the Gunfighter is shared with those younger ones who yearn to go to the sound of the musketry. The Gunfighter is remembered and honored by those who really count—other Gunfighters.

And therein lies the real reward to America's finest sons—Her Gunfighters.

Gene does an outstanding job depicting our United States Marine warriors, gunfighters in every sense of the word. His military occupational specialty might be refrigeration repairman or administrative chief, but if he is a Marine, he is a gunfighter. What follows are the stories of several of these gunfighters, the Marine leaders on my flank.

Although Corporal Myron Davis, my squad leader in the Korean War, and Major General George W. Smith, my battalion commander in the Vietnam War, fit well within the theme and purpose of this chapter, they were my leaders but not on my flank. Those commanders they did flank surely appreciated having their support. I covered both leaders and their manner of leadership in earlier chapters.

SERGEANT SHELTON LEE EAKIN

After Corporal Myron Davis, the next most impressive Marine I encountered in my Marine Corps life was Sergeant Shelton Lee Eakin. We had much in common. We not only had the same middle name, but he was another southerner. Eakin was from Arkansas. But it was more than that. We had the same ideas as to what being a Marine was all about. Shelton didn't join the Marines because he was an average young man; he stood out among his peers during his growing up years, or he at least was aware of the desire to do so. He learned of the Marines, the few, the proud, the gunfighters, and because of his personal goals, he decided to join. He knew it wouldn't be easy in 1952, but he took it on; he would be a Marine. The making of a Marine is a tough road for many young people, but the end results are that one is a Marine for life and has the satisfaction of service to his country as a gunfighter.

Eakin was the first Marine I knew who, like me, wanted as his position the Marine infantry occupational field as his first choice; he would have no other. We had the same thoughts on all issues confronting us, and if possible, he was even more gung-ho than I.

In the early 1950s few Marines joined the Marine Corps as their first choice upon leaving or graduating from high school. Though the fighting in Korea had been replaced with peace talks by 1954, the Selective Service draft continued into the 1970s. The majority of those in uniform, all uniforms, were there because of the draft. All young men knew that they were going to be in a military uniform sooner or later. Even though the Marines didn't get many who had received their notice and were drafted, the draft was the drive, the motivator: Sign up now or . . . Those who were in Marine uniform as their first choice, for the most part, were noticeable in their motivation and performance of duty, as well as in the maintenance of their uniforms, compared to others in the ranks, and Sergeant Eakin stood out. He was a Marine by choice, right out of high school.

We first met in October 1955, when I checked into George Company, 3rd Battalion, 5th Marine Regiment, 1st Marine Division in Korea. Eakin was young, not yet twenty-one, and he was a slick-arm buck sergeant (E-4), meaning that he didn't have fours years of active duty in the Corps under his belt: The term "slick-arm" came from the fact that he didn't wear the hash mark on his uniform representing four years of Marine Corps service. At this time I was an old salt; I had been wearing the hash mark for three months. Eakin was the platoon sergeant of the 3rd Rifle Platoon, George Company, 3rd Battalion. I had the 2nd Platoon, and we were always in competition with our platoons— which was a good thing!

One of the first things I noticed upon checking in to George Company and settling down to leadership business, was the fact that regardless of Eakin's youthful appearance and easy, friendly manner of dealing with and handling his Marines, he was always addressed as Sergeant Eakin. My rifle company experience of earlier years, when the old salts addressed their corporals and sergeants by last name only, was fresh in my mind. After my time in Item

Company, I kept my distance from my Marines so as not to become "Fox." I wanted to hear "Sergeant Fox." I learned a lot from my slick-arm buddy.

Shelton loved and was good in sports, especially football. I observed him out there in the rice paddies with his Marines, playing "hard ball." He would clobber one, get the ball, and take off, only to be nailed by half a dozen of his Marines. Yelling and cussing one another, they were covered with mud, sweat, and blood, but they had fun. To a man, they loved the tough, physical contact: They were a team. And it was obvious that they loved their leader and that they had the greatest respect for him. He was always addressed as Sergeant Eakin. I was learning a new page in Marine leadership.

In spite of what I had learned about Shelton's leadership and the respect he received from his Marines, I was still surprised to see him placed one day in a fifty-five-gallon fire barrel of water, head first. We had just received the word that our 5th Marine Regiment would go on board ships within two weeks for our return to the States. Sergeant Eakin passed that word to his platoon members, as we all did, and his Marines instantly grabbed him, carried him to a fire barrel beside their tent, and dunked him in. They must have done it several times as I was able to get a picture of it with his boots high in the air over the barrel and his Marine's shoulders. They were celebrating the word.

Eakin and I next served together as drill instructors at the Marine Corps Recruit Depot in San Diego, although we were in different battalions. I know he made some great Marines, and I have met a few in the Corps who had nothing but good things to say about their drill instructor. Our next time together was in 1st Force Reconnaissance Company at Camp Pendleton, California. Eakin, now a staff sergeant (E-6), had joined 1st Force while I was on recruiting duty back East, and through him I learned of my choice for my next duty station. Shelton gave me the "road map" of how to get into this new, elite organization, and I followed it closely. The details of our 1st Force Reconnaissance Company experience are covered in my memoir. Shelton was the platoon sergeant of one of the reconnaissance platoons, and I became the platoon sergeant of the Pathfinder Platoon.

A night parachute operation highlights this Marine leader's presence of mind, abilities, and concern for others. Eakin had exited the jump aircraft, and as his parachute inflated, the Marine exiting the plane behind him fell by Eakin. That recon Marine's chute had failed to open for whatever reason; he fell very close beside Eakin, with his unopened parachute dragging behind his falling body and rubbing against Eakin's body. Eakin quickly realized what was happening. He was able to grab the malfunctioned parachute in the dark of night and hold on to it until they hit the ground, eight hundred feet below. He saved that young Marine's life, an action for which he was later awarded the Navy and Marine Corps Medal.

I saw Shelton Eakin only once after our 1st Force Recon days, when he was stationed at Marine Barracks, 8th and I Street, Washington, D.C. I was on my way to Paris and a billet at Supreme Headquarters, Allied Powers, Europe. En route my family enjoyed a warm visit with Eakin and his family in his home in Maryland.

As gunnery sergeants in 1965, Eakin was stationed at our Marine Barracks in Washington, D.C., with the duty as the color sergeant in all parades, and I was the Security and Honor Guard platoon sergeant in Supreme Headquarters, Allied Powers, Europe. Due to the needs of the Marine Corps (also covered in my memoir), we were both temporarily commissioned to second lieutenants in 1966. Within a month Lieutenant Eakin was assigned to Vietnam, and knowing him, I know he worked that out with a personal contact at the Marine Corps Personnel Assignment section. He was assigned to a reconnaissance battalion in Vietnam and was killed within a month of arriving in country.

Lieutenant Eakin was on his third reconnaissance patrol. His team had been inserted by helicopter into a landing zone, and typical of Shelton, he led his team off of the chopper and into the bush. He had not moved fifty yards into the brush when he hit a mine or booby trap that removed everything, including his hips, downward. The chopper was still on the ground; his team members gathered him up and placed him on the chopper, which flew him directly out to a naval hospital ship. In spite of the loss of most of his body, he lived several hours on the hospital ship. His last words were to his family, his wife and young son. That was Shelton Lee Eakin. One hell of a Marine and leader. I learned of Eakin's final hours from his company commander at the time, Captain Timothy Geraghty, who flew out to the ship as soon as he learned of the team's fate.

SECOND LIEUTENANT WILLIAM J. CHRISTMAN III

Though Second Lieutenant William J. Christman III was young, with only a year in the Marine Corps, he had it all worked out. Leading was easy for him because he was a natural leader with a personality that fit that task. In 1968, I was the commander of Alpha Company, 1st Battalion, 9th Marines, a rifle company in combat in northern I Corps, Vietnam. During December of that year, I was joined by three young lieutenants fresh from the Basic School, where Marine lieutenants learn how to handle, lead, and fight with a Marine rifle platoon. I needed them because three of my officers had completed their six months of rifle company combat time and were due to depart.

One of these new lieutenants was Bill Christman, who presented himself to me in a pleasant, friendly manner supported with direct eye contact. He had a solid, muscular build, was about five feet nine inches tall, and weighed about 190 pounds. His blond hair was almost invisible due to his short (to the skin) Marine haircut. He looked the part of a football player, and he later entertained us with stories of some of his college fun games.

I was impressed by how he had presented himself to me during my interview. I liked his response to my questions, his direct eye contact as we talked, and the pleasure he took in having duty with the Marine Corps in Vietnam. His highest hope was to receive command of a rifle platoon, the dream of all real Marine 2nd lieutenants, tomorrow's gunfighters. He had done well at the Basic School with his focus on leading Marine infantry in combat. I assigned Bill as the platoon leader of my 3rd Rifle Platoon.

Bill wanted the platoon leadership position and task, but think about the challenges and questions that had to be in that young man's mind. There were, of course, the normal thoughts that come to all first-time commanders anywhere: How will my Marines accept me and respond to my direction and orders? How well will I handle my duties as the leader under enemy fire? He must also have given thought to how he would personally handle and react to combat, to being under fire with his future, his life, at stake. Gunfighters, however, don't dwell on that last thought.

To state that Bill did well is an oversimplification of major proportion. He did all of the right things required of positive leadership, and he quickly became an important focus for his Marines, a member as well as the leader of the team. His Marines always referred to him as "my lieutenant," and they quickly placed him in that singular position of "someone who cares about me." When there was work to do—digging fighting holes, clearing fields of fire, whatever—Bill got sweaty. He was still the leader, he provided the guidance and direction, but he didn't do it while standing around with his hands on his hips or in his pockets.

Lieutenant Bill Christman made total commitment to his Marines, his command, and the Corps. What was in the best interest of his Marines was always foremost in his mind; his Marines knew that they mattered to him, that he cared about them. Care: that most essential element of leadership.

I usually found Bill on the line at night when I went out to check my company positions and to ensure that those Marines on watch were awake and alert. Bill was always somewhere within his platoon's frontage; he wasn't talking with his Marines or in any other way detrimental to our security. He was there providing physical support to the young men on watch, to let them know that he cared, that he was involved. I checked my lines at a different time each night, but it didn't matter. Bill was almost always out there. I told him I was concerned that he wasn't getting enough rest and sleep, and that it was important that the commander not be exhausted should we be assaulted. He told me he got enough sleep. I don't know how, though, because he was always out there on the line.

We were on Operation Dewey Canyon in the A Shau Valley when Lieutenant Christman really stood out from the average Marine lieutenant. Our battalion had been on the operation about two weeks, we had just captured two big 155-mm Russian artillery guns, and my Alpha Company had continued the attack down our ridgeline to the Laotian border and our Objective Foxtrot. Charlie Company and Headquarters and Service Company with our battalion command group had remained with the captured guns, behind us. Battalion's problem was waiting for our higher echelon leaders to determine if and what helicopter was required to lift the big guns out of the valley. The guns were in good condition and operational, and higher commanders wanted to save them, to lift them out of the jungle if possible.

Enemy activity to the flank of the guns and Charlie Company's position caused the battalion commander to consider the fact that the North Vietnamese Army commander might be planning to recover the guns. I received a radio message from Colonel Smith: "Hammer Hand, send your best rifle platoon back to my position. I have a mission for them." The colonel went on to explain that he had to determine what the enemy force might be up to and what its strength was. Company C could not provide a platoon for the mission as it took the entire company to provide security around the guns and around Headquarters and Service Company, especially if they were about to be under attack.

I gave Bill the mission and told him to take his platoon with attached machine guns back to battalion. He was to report to Colonel Smith for details on the mission, which amounted to a reconnaissance/combat patrol. True to form Bill and my 3rd Platoon did all of that, including locating the enemy force where it was thought to be. My 3rd Platoon locked into the North Vietnamese Army unit only to learn that they were a bigger and stronger force.

Bill realized that he could not overcome the enemy force that was defending with machine guns and automatic rifles. He wanted to break contact and withdraw his platoon. However, he had several Marines down under the enemy's guns, and he would not leave without all of his Marines. Each time he would raise his volume of fire to suppress the enemy gunfire so he could recover his Marine casualties, naturally the enemy thought he was assaulting and heavily increased their weapons fire. Bill tried to recover his Marines several times without success. But he wasn't leaving without them. Darkness fell and that gave him his chance. For whatever reason the enemy did not interfere with his recovery attempts in the darkness. He recovered his Marines and returned to the ridge top, where I also had rejoined the battalion command with Alpha Company.

Earlier, when Colonel Smith learned by radio from Lieutenant Christman of 3rd Platoon's problem, he had called me with directions to return with Alpha Company to his position. The enemy force really had his attention now, and he would send Alpha Company down the following day to take care of the problem. Alpha arrived at the battalion position late in the evening of 21 February 1969. Bill and his 3rd Platoon joined me there much later, and he was noticeably bothered when he learned of our mission the following day.

Bill didn't agree with my thought that the North Vietnamese Army personnel would not be there tomorrow. My experience had been that they never stayed in the same place where they had been located by us, and for a good reason. We would pound the daylights out of them with supporting arms, artillery, and air assaults. And we did just that; we fired artillery all night into that valley and brought in night bomber aircraft on the target. But as we would learn the following day, in that jungle we didn't know the target's exact location. Our maps were not that good, and there were no terrain features for reference, just dense jungle. The stuff we threw at them didn't even get close. Bill was correct. We would have a major fight on our hands for an understrength Marine rifle company.

We located the enemy force on 22 February 1969, and we had a touch-and-go battle for the better part of the afternoon, as I described in an earlier chapter. Our nation, our Corps, and my 3rd Rifle Platoon lost a great young leader that day. Bill was hit by machine-gun fire early in that fight as he led his platoon of Marines forward into the enemy's well-positioned machine guns. Though he was down with several machine-gun bullets through his chest, he didn't die until we were carrying him up the mountain that night after the fight was over.

Lieutenant William Christman's personal actions were notable based on what he and his rifle platoon accomplished. I personally know what he accomplished and how he handled it, though I was never within eyesight of him. That dense jungle foliage reduced observation to only the Marine on each side of you.

The jungle and the casualties taken (eleven killed in that action and fifty-four of my Marines wounded and medevaced out on the twenty-third due to the threat of loss of life or limb) took away all eyewitness to individual valorous action. I wanted to write Bill up for the Medal of Honor because what he did and what he accomplished was surely deserving of it. But I could not get the required two eyewitnesses to support the recommendation. My recommendation was downgraded to the Navy Cross, which his wife and daughter later received.

What follows is an excerpt from Lieutenant Christman's Navy Cross citation:

> [He] skillfully maneuvered his men forward in a coordinated attack until halted and pinned down by the extremely heavy volume of cross fire from the North Vietnamese emplacements and numerous sniper positions in trees. He directed the fire of his machine guns and light antitank weapons against the North Vietnamese emplacements and mounted such an aggressive assault that his platoon moved through the forward enemy positions. Undaunted by the enemy rounds impacting around him, he fired his light antitank assault weapon, and fearlessly charging across the fire-swept terrain, hurled hand grenades into a hostile emplacement, killing seven North Vietnamese soldiers and silencing their machine gun. Coming under fire from an adjacent bunker, he was mortally wounded while attempting to fire his light antitank assault weapon against the emplacement. With his remaining strength, he resolutely propped himself up on one arm to direct his men in outflanking and destroying the enemy bunker.

FIRST LIEUTENANT LEE ROY HERRON

I knew First Lieutenant Lee Roy Herron for only two months, but two months in combat is a long time. Six feet plus in height and muscular in build, Lee wore eyeglasses, and he presented a warm, friendly face to all he encountered. He was a personable guy, one who enjoyed the company of others, and he was always quick to do for them. He never uttered a profane word, and at the same time he fit in with and was quickly accepted into all circles. Lee had spent the year since graduating from the Basic School at Monterey, California, learning Vietnamese. He wouldn't need the language out in the bush with us, but he would use the leadership principles and skills he learned at the Basic School.

Lieutenant Herron joined Alpha Company shortly after Christmas 1968, and as a first lieutenant, I assigned him the duty of Alpha Company's executive officer, the next in command. Rifle company executive officers normally handle the administration and paperwork for the commander.

Lee, right off, made it clear that he wanted to get involved in our company activities. He wanted action; he was a gunfighter at heart. I suggested that he could help me check the lines at night because I had become concerned my second night in command after finding the watch in a machine-gun team asleep in a bunker (the story is covered in my memoir). Not only was this Marine asleep, but he was in a bunker with the door propped shut and his rifle placed against the door on the outside from him. How bad is that? (In the Korean War the gun teams were the only ones that could be counted upon to have someone awake.) I had a serious company security problem, and I was spending a large part of my nights moving along my line. And as you might expect, one doesn't just skip along and whistle while moving on a Marine combat front line in the darkness of night and usually in jungle-type vegetation. I divided our company defensive line in half, Lee's part and mine.

Lee eagerly took on the task of night line checks. As a matter of fact, I found him on my half so often that I began to wonder (like I did with Bill Christman) when he got his rest. He didn't visit with the Marines on watch and talk but sat there quietly in the dark, one position after another, providing that command interest and support (care). As a matter of fact, I found Lee on the line so often that I felt we were doing an overkill. I suggested that we take turns, only one of us each night. He was to do the lines every other night. He insisted that he was getting enough sleep, and he needed something to do. I continued to find him on the line on my night, so I backed off. I gave him the total line-check duty, and I got more sleep. Lee and Bill both being on the line at night took away my concern for our security. All watch standers had the word: "You had better be awake and alert!"

Lee also was very much involved with his Marines spiritually. I was aware that he shared his time with our God, and Lee's beliefs were deep-seated. As our battalion crossed the line of departure in our movement forward on Operation

Dewey Canyon in the A Shau Valley, our battalion chaplain had declared himself a heat casualty. Before we left our first night position, and very convenient for him, he walked to our helicopter landing zone to catch the next bird out. He had told our battalion commander that he could not continue with the operation, that he was overcome by heat. (Maybe, it was a warm night, and sleeping does use some energy, but the days surely got hotter for the rest of us.) My rifle company was last off the hill, and we walked by that chaplain standing with his head down in the landing zone as our battalion moved into our attack.

Lee always brought up the rear of my company during our movements while I was at the front, so I wasn't with him as he passed that chaplain on the landing zone. But I know it hit him hard to see a man of the cloth quit on us. One-nine went in the attack without our official chaplain, but we had a man of the Lord with us. Lee assumed the responsibility on his own and went above and beyond the call of duty to arrange and hold spiritual meetings. He assured that counseling was available to all Marines who wanted it. Lee on occasions was able to get a helicopter to carry our Marines who wanted Sunday service to another unit's area where a chaplain was conducting services.

Lee's last hour on earth was during our attack into the North Vietnamese Army position in the A Shau Valley on 22 February. My two assault rifle platoons had been stopped by heavy machine-gun fire, and I had made the decision to commit my reserve rifle platoon. As I completed my order to that platoon commander, Lieutenant James Davis, a mortar round hit among us, seriously wounding Jim Davis. Lee had heard my order to Jim; I asked if he had any questions concerning the order and told him to take the 2nd Platoon in the attack. Lee did just that in typical Basic School form: hand over head with a sweeping forward motion and the words "Follow me."

Lee did not have much help because that platoon was so small that there was little hope that it would make a difference. It was the one that several hours earlier had suffered two casualties and provided the rifle squad that carried and escorted the casualties and the water detail up the mountain. I did not feel good about our chances with fewer than twenty Marines getting our assault moving forward again, but I did not allow for the superb efforts of the officer leading that assault.

The movement forward by 2nd Platoon caused an increase in heavy enemy weapons fire, but soon their machine-gun fire was noticeably reduced. But Lee had made a difference at a high price. I received a radio call from the platoon sergeant, Sergeant David A. Beyerlein, that Lieutenant Herron had been cut down by machine-gun fire. Lee's action, nevertheless, got my company assault moving again. We attacked through and secured the enemy position.

I was so impressed with the changes in the enemy's posture resulting from Lee's assault that I initially wrote him up for the Medal of Honor. Two eyewitnesses are a prerequisite for that award, and the next day I found no one around who had been involved with or saw Lee's action. We were in thick jungle with a heavy mist of rain continually moving through the trees. Those directly involved with Lee had either been killed or seriously wounded and medevaced to the rear the next morning.

I knew what had to have taken place, but I did not see it. I pieced together what those of us present knew Lee had to have done for the results we received in that battle. Lieutenant Lee Roy Herron's family received the Navy Cross, which he was awarded for his action on 22 February 1969.

What follows is an excerpt from Lieutenant Lee Roy Herron's Navy Cross citation:

Aware that the fire from two mutually supporting hostile machine guns was holding his Marines in place and preventing the removal of the casualties, he completely disregarded his own safety as he exposed himself to North Vietnamese fire to direct a light antitank assault round which scored a direct hit on one of the machine gun bunkers. Boldly leaping to his feet, he fearlessly charged across the fire-swept terrain to hurl hand grenades and fire his weapon against the enemy emplacement, killing nine North Vietnamese soldiers who were in the bunker. While directing his men in the assault on the remaining bunker, First Lieutenant Herron was mortally wounded.

Lee Roy Herron will always be thought of as a motivated, can-do young Marine leader because of the scholarship memorial established in his name at his Texas Tech University. I and about a dozen old Alpha Company, One-Nine Marines gathered for the scholarship dedication in his honor several years ago. The event, initiated and supported by Lee's lifetime buddy, Marine David Nelson, supplied closure in the memory of one great young Marine leader and gunfighter. I give my deep-felt thanks to David and Texas Tech for all they have done in Lee's memory. Lee was technically and tactically proficient in everything he encountered. When I think of leadership, I think of Lee Roy Herron, a Texan and a Marine who cared.

CAPTAIN EDWARD RILEY

Captain Edward Riley was the commander of Delta Company at the time I had Alpha Company in the Vietnamese War. Ed was a quiet, serious, and involved mustang Marine leader. (Mustang is the name given to Marine officers who served as enlisted Marines prior to being commissioned, which is at least a third, if not more, of Marine officers.) I was in the battalion about two months before I met Ed, the same with my meeting other battalion officers, because we were in the bush, meaning operational and usually within our own company tactical area of operations. There was no enemy force large enough for higher commanders to be concerned that a Marine rifle company couldn't handle it. Then came Christmas 1968, and we all collected at Vandegrift Combat Base for the holiday.

There I met most of our battalion officers, including our battalion XO, Major C. D. Foreman, our operations officer, Major D. N. Kennon, and my fellow rifle company commanders. The three rifle company commanders, though captains, accepted me with my lieutenant rank as an equal, which pleased me. Captain George Meerdink Jr. had Bravo Company, Captain John "Blackjack" Kelly had Charlie Company, and Ed had Delta. We were brothers, solid members of Lieutenant Colonel George W. Smith's battalion team, and we knew we were blessed with the best in the Marine warrior business.

Up to this point we had known each other only by radio call signs when keeping abreast of what was happening with our sister companies on our flanks through radio traffic. Now each call sign had not only a face but also a personality. I was very much impressed with the men holding the leadership positions within our battalion. Little did I know that within two months we would all get a chance to take it to the nth degree and two would lose their lives.

Ed's Delta Company had come to my attention several weeks earlier with the "bug out" of his company gunnery sergeant (this story is covered in my two earlier books). I respected Ed for his manner of handling that issue but really got to know the man at Vandegrift.

Another point that impressed me about this Marine leader was his personal integrity, which was expressed with his interpretation of and manner of handling the enemy body count. As I noted earlier, our supporting arms leaders required a body count for all of the support provided to us, and it was difficult for us to comply short of walking through the area and counting the bodies. Ed refused to give a number of enemy dead and would state specifically why— usually because he had no eyeballs in the area and it would be only a guess: "If a guess of the body count is what you want, put down a figure that you choose. But I won't support it."

Operation Dewey Canyon had Bravo and Delta Companies on a ridgeline to the right of the one that Charlie Company, our Headquarters and Service Company, and my company were attacking down toward Laos. We all had some good contacts, including ambushes on some of our squad patrols working on our flanks, enemy night assaults against our positions, and our overrunning and capturing the two enemy 155-mm artillery pieces. (One of these is in the new Marine Corps Museum by our Quantico Marine Corps Base, and the Army has the other one at Fort Sill, their artillery base.) Ed and I hit Laos on separate ridges at about the same time, and he moved east to join me on Objective Foxtrot. Only I wasn't there to welcome him.

Colonel Smith had directed me to return to his position. Alpha Company would take care of the enemy force he thought was preparing to recapture the two enemy artillery pieces (to which he had earlier committed my 3rd Rifle Platoon with Lieutenant Bill Christman). Both Christman's fight on the twenty-first and mine on the twenty-second were covered earlier; here I want to focus on Ed Riley.

Ed received the word by radio from Colonel Smith to move to my aid in the valley below him. His first thoughts were that Alpha Company needed help now, and he had to have his Marines break camp, pack up, and move out. That takes time. Plus he had to find a route through the jungle to get to us. How? How could he get there in time to be of help to Alpha? He and his Marines had heard the heavy weapons fire going on in the valley below, and they expected that Alpha Marines were hurting and could use their help.

As he talked on the radio with Colonel Smith, Ed was surprised to see his Marines with their gear on their backs and their rifles on their shoulders standing in formation on the trail. His company was ready to move to sister Alpha's aid, now. On their own they had broken camp and packed up and were ready to fight with Alpha Company Marines. Ed didn't bother with his gear. He left it. He grabbed his war belt and helmet and moved Delta toward the sounds of the guns.

Ed was correct: The fight was over when he joined me in that valley, but Alpha needed Delta's help anyway. Alpha Company had more casualties than it could carry. One of Delta Company's rifle platoons was provided to help carry our casualties up that mountain to the ridge where Charlie Company and Headquarters and Service Company were positioned. Ed had the rest of his Marines collect all of the enemy's weapons and ordnance, as well as my casualties' weapons, and destroy them. He was several hours in accomplishing this and didn't reach us on the ridge until well after midnight.

Captain Riley and his Marines, in addition to ensuring that no Marine was left in the valley, provided a body count of the enemy dead. I was surprised the next day to learn the figure of 105 enemy soldiers killed in that action. But that explains why it was touch and go for Alpha Company there for a while. We were greatly outnumbered considering our role as the aggressor. But when the aggressors are Marine gunfighters, they will be the winners. When Ed stated that the body count was 105, it was 105.

Delta Company's next task was taking Hill 1044, southeast of Objective Foxtrot, the hill that was to get a lot of Marine focus and attention over the next several weeks. The North Vietnamese Army forces holding 1044 put up a strong defense, but Ed's two-platoon assault got the best of them. This hill was along the Vietnam-Laos border but it was on the Vietnamese side. The side toward Laos had been cleared pretty well of vegetation by our Air Force B-52 bombing runs, and that fact provided our next entertainment.

One of Delta's Marines needed to relieve his bowels. He took his entrenching tool and headed for the bottom of one of those five-hundred-pound bomb craters. He didn't get much of a hole dug because below several inches of dirt, he hit wooden boxes. It turned out that the North Vietnamese Army's weapons and supplies were buried in the bottom of most of the bomb craters. My Alpha Company moved over to help Delta dig up and destroy all of those weapons and ordnance, which turned out to be a major job lasting several days for our entire battalion.

All of my Marines came away with a personal war trophy, a new SKS semi-automatic Chinese-made rifle. That gave me some concern. I wondered how well they could fight with a second rifle on their shoulders, but they deserved the rifles and they wanted them, so they kept them.

Finally, with suitable flying weather, the time came to get the Walking Death Battalion out of the A Shau Valley. Delta Company was the last to be lifted out of the Dewey Canyon operation, and Ed was not yet finished. His rifle platoons had boarded choppers and were airborne and headed for Vandegrift. Ed, after checking to make sure that all of his Marines had been accounted for and were gone, boarded the last chopper with his command group. As they lifted off and gained altitude, Ed happened to look though a porthole and see two of his Marines running down a finger on the ridge toward the helicopter landing zone. Damn, he thought, how did they not get the word to move to the zone earlier? There was nothing to do except turn the chopper around, land, and get those two Marines. They did that without suffering any enemy action, and Ed joined us at Vandegrift Combat Base. Marines take care of Marines, and there is no limit, no end to that care.

The leaders serving on my flank were not only in combat situations but were in our every-day Marine life. I want to again emphasize that there were many Marines on my flank in combat in both wars who are not included in this book. The reason is that my focus here is leadership and those individuals were gun-fighters. Charles "Chuck" Hudson, my senior corpsman in Alpha Company One-Nine, Vietnam, is an example of such a marine, as are Estel Tuggle and John Hall of Item Company, 3rd Battalion, 5th Marines in Korea. While there were many Marines who fit this category, I will write about one here, one who stood out in every way as a Marine leader and gunfighter covering my flank—though we never served together in combat.

COLONEL JOHN WALTER RIPLEY

I first met First Lieutenant John Walter Ripley in 2nd Force Reconnaissance Company at Camp Lejeune, North Carolina, in 1966. I reported in as a new second lieutenant looking forward to my first duty as an officer. The company commander informed me that I would take command of the 2nd Force Reconnaissance Platoon and followed with sending a runner to bring Lieutenant Ripley to his office. I was pleased upon meeting John. His warm personality, direct eye contact, and physical appearance fit that of a young Marine leader. John was on a short fuse the day I met him. He was checking out of the company en route to duty in Vietnam. He sent word to have his platoon fall in, and I followed him to the formation.

John thanked his Marines for their service and for their dedication to their reconnaissance platoon mission and to him. He informed them that he was departing for the Vietnam War within the hour and wanted to shake each recon Marine's hand. He followed with introducing me as their new platoon commander, and he told them he knew they would serve Lieutenant Fox in the same manner as they had served him. He shook each Marine's hand warmly with a clap on their shoulder and departed.

John served in Vietnam as the commander of Lima Company, 3rd Battalion, 3rd Marines in the Marine "up-front" manner as I have discussed. This was typical of John; he was always involved with his Marines. He was wounded in action and received the Silver Star Medal for valorous action as well as the Purple Heart.

I next met John when I was home on a thirty-day leave, which I had received for extending my tour of duty time in Vietnam. I realized that I could maybe influence my duty assignment following my Vietnam tour by visiting my duty assignment monitor in Headquarters Marine Corps. Dressed in my squared away service Alpha uniform, I did that; I discovered which room I should go to and walked in.

A young man in a business suit standing in the room looked at me and asked, "How badly did you mess up my 2nd Force Reconnaissance Platoon?" For a second I couldn't imagine what this civilian was talking about; was he talking to me? Then I recognized John. The suit had thrown me off. All military personnel serving in the Washington, D.C., area at that time had to wear civilian clothes four days each week. I understand that the reason was to mislead those who might be counting the number of military personnel assigned to the Washington area.

John, in his friendly, concerned manner, was interested in helping me with a duty station and provided sound advice. My choice was Camp Pendleton, California, and 1st Force Reconnaissance Company, but John pointed out that because my family was in our Leesburg home, which was within the commute distance to Quantico, I might want to go to the Amphibious Warfare School (AWS) located at Quantico. Graduation from AWS then only took six months, and it was followed with a permanent unit assignment. That would save me two household moves within a year at a later time by not having to come to Quantico for only six months.

As I was a temporary officer, I never considered being eligible for officer schooling and responded with that thought. John answered, "There is nothing in my directives that prevent you from going to Amphibious Warfare School. I submit a list of recommended captains based on their fitness reports and that is the only requirement. You are as qualified as any other captain." He looked at my record and confirmed his opinion. "That is what I recommend."

"Thanks, John, put me down for it. I'll do the school following my Vietnam assignment, and I appreciate your help."

Captain Ripley's next assignment was as an infantry battalion advisor with the Vietnamese Marine Corps. His battalion was in defensive positions just south of the Cam Lo-Cua Viet River when the North Vietnamese Army assaulted southward in March 1972. As the heavy enemy tank unit—two hundred T-54 tanks and thirty thousand enemy troops—moved toward them, John realized that the bridge over the river had to be destroyed. With the enemy tank force on the north side of that Dong Ha Bridge firing across the river, John, with the help of one Army officer, Major James E. Smock, managed to drop the bridge in front of them and hold up their assault. John's story is told by two authors, Colonel Gerry H. Turley in his book *The Easter Offensive* and Colonel John Miller in his book *The Bridge at Dong Ha.*

As John's actions were in full view of enemy forces and under enemy fire, I have never accepted the fact that he was not deserving of the Medal of Honor. His actions were above and beyond the call of duty, but the requirement for two eyewitnesses may have been a consideration in his not getting the medal. I understand that Major Smock was not available as a witness to those commanders later writing up the award recommendation. However, there were Vietnamese Marines who witnessed the bridge destruction, and there were many other ways to determine that the bridge was gone. John was not wounded during the action, but that is not a requirement for the Medal of Honor. Two Marines I know received the medal and were not wounded during their particular heroic action in the Vietnam War. John deserved the Medal of Honor, but he was awarded the Navy Cross.

Since meeting John Ripley in 1966, I have been involved with him continually, though we only served together in a Marine unit for one day. He invited me to the Naval Academy several times to talk leadership with his Marine-option midshipmen when he was the senior Marine there. He along with Jim Webb was responsible for causing the Marine Corps to require midshipmen who wished to be Marines to go through the Marine Corps Officer Candidates School at Quantico. Their justification was that academy midshipmen were behind other lieutenants going through the Basic School. The problem was that there were Marine Corps subjects and issues that lieutenants learned at OCS of which midshipmen were unaware. The midshipmen had to play hard catch-up ball, and who should know that better than John and Jim. They had been there, done that.

The OCS requirement for midshipmen wanting to be Marines happened during my time at the school, and I was surprised at the number of midshipmen DORs (those who "drop on request") that it caused. Some midshipmen didn't want to be a Marine leader after all, not at that price. The Navy didn't like this approach either because they had to commission the Marine Corps rejects.

That routine only lasted for three years before another way was found to get midshipmen up on the power curve. I cover this issue fully in my memoir.

John and I spent much time together over the years, often with our wives, Moline and Dotti Lu. We were members of several associations, such as Force Reconnaissance, the Vietnamese Advisor, and the Marine Corps Law Enforcement Foundation. I never missed a chance to spend time with my buddy, another Marine covering my flank. His son, Tom, went through Officer Candidates School while I was the commander there; I enjoyed that connection very much.

John wrote a book review on my *Marine Rifleman: Forty-three Years in the Corps* for the *Marine Corps Gazette*. The same month this issue of the *Gazette* hit the book stands, John underwent a major operation: the replacement of his liver. How could he read the book and write the review while feeling so badly? He had to have been awfully sick while involved in that work, but that was John. He took care of others; his family and friends came first.

Our country, our Corps, his family, and his friends lost John in November 2008. He is now in charge of and working with those Marines guarding the gates in heaven. He is also going to be with Marines in our Marine Corps for many years to come, as are all other great Marines who have left so much here on Earth for us to remember and pass on to our young followers. Another way to spell "leadership" is John Walter Ripley.

Sources

Burkett, B. G., and Glenna Whitley. *Stolen Valor: How the Vietnam Generation Was Robbed of Its Heroes and Its History.* Dallas: Verity Press, 1998.

Covey, Stephen. *The Seven Habits of Highly Effective People.* New York: Free Press, 1989.

Drucker, Peter F. *Managing the Non-Profit Organization: Principles and Practices.* New York: HarperCollins, 1990.

Finzell, Hans. *The Top Ten Mistakes Leaders Make.* Colorado Springs, Colo.: David C. Cook, 2007.

Fox, Wesley L. *Courage and Fear.* Dulles, Va.: Potomac Books, 2007.

———. *Marine Rifleman: Forty-three Years in the Corps.* Dulles, Va.: Potomac Books, 2002.

McMichael, Sgt. Maj. Alford L. *Leadership: Achieving Life-Changing Success from Within.* New York: Threshold Editions, 2008.

Miller, John. *The Bridge at Dong Ha.* Annapolis: Naval Institute Press, 1996.

Myers, Col. Donald. *Leadership Defined.* Baltimore: Gateway Press, 1999.

Patterson, Lt. Col. Robert. *Dereliction of Duty: The Eyewitness Account of How Bill Clinton Compromised America's National Security.* Washington, D.C.: Regnery, 2003.

Sallah, Michael, and Mitch Weiss. *Tiger Force: A True Story of Men and War.* Boston: Little, Brown, 2006.

Smith, Maj. Gen. Perry M. *Rules and Tools for Leaders: A Down-to-Earth Guide to Effective Managing.* New York: Perigee, 2002.

Taylor, Robert L., and William E. Rosenbach. *Military Leadership: In Pursuit of Excellence.* Boulder, Colo.: Westview Press, 2005.

Turley, Col. Gerry H. *The Easter Offensive: The Last American Advisors, Vietnam 1972.* Novato, Calif.: Presidio Press, 1985.

Useem , Michael. *Leading Up: How to Lead Your Boss So You Both Win.* New York: Three Rivers Press, 2001.

Von Schell, Capt. Adolf, and Maj. Edwin F. Harding. *Battle Leadership.* Quantico, Va.: Marine Corps Association,1982.

Index

About the Author

COL. WESLEY L. FOX joined the Marines in 1950, serving in the Korean War. Commissioned a lieutenant in 1966, he served as an adviser with the Vietnamese marines. He later commanded a U.S. Marine rifle company and was involved in an action that resulted in his being awarded the Medal of Honor. His last active duty was as Commanding Officer, Officer Candidate School, where he retired in 1993.